THE 360 LIBRARIAN

A Framework for Integrating MINDFULNESS, EMOTIONAL INTELLIGENCE, and CRITICAL REFLECTION in the Workplace

Tammi M. Owens and
Carol A. Daul-Elhindi

Association of College and Research Libraries
A division of the American Library Association
Chicago, Illinois 2020

The paper used in this publication meets the minimum requirements of American National Standard for Information Sciences–Permanence of Paper for Printed Library Materials, ANSI Z39.48-1992. ∞

Library of Congress Control Number:2019955025

Copyright ©2020 by the Association of College and Research Libraries.

All rights reserved except those which may be granted by Sections 107 and 108 of the Copyright Revision Act of 1976.

Printed in the United States of America.

1 2 3 4 5 24 23 22 21 20

Dedications

To my husband, Scott Owens, my one true love. Thank you for teaching me how to live in this moment.

I dedicate this book to my husband, Dr. Mohamed Elhindi, for his endless support and to my son, Solomon Elhindi, for his guidance from above.

Table of Contents

iii .... Dedications

vii .... Preface

1 .... **Part 1. Building a Framework of 360 Librarian Ideals**

        3 .... **Introduction**

        13 .... **Chapter 1.** Mindful Practice

        27 .... **Chapter 2.** Emotional Awareness

        41 .... **Chapter 3.** Engaged Communication

        55 .... **Chapter 4.** Empathetic Reflection and Action

        69 .... **Chapter 5.** Reassurance

83 .... **Part 2. Implementing an Intentional 360 Librarian Practice**

        85 .... **Introduction**

        87 .... **Chapter 6.** 360 Librarian Practice While Consulting with Students

        97 .... **Chapter 7.** 360 Librarian Practice in the Information Literacy Classroom

        113 ...... **Chapter 8.** 360 Librarian Practice in Reaching Out and Marketing the Library

        123 ...... **Chapter 9.** 360 Librarian Practice in Working with Technology

        131 ...... **Chapter 10.** 360 Librarian Practice in Leadership

141 ...... Bibliography

147 ...... Author Biographies

149 ...... Index

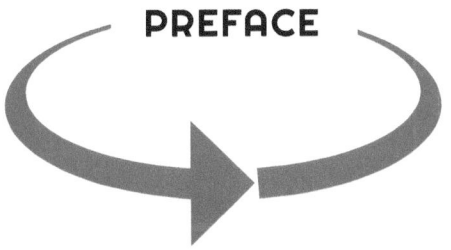

Preface

The 360 Librarian is the result of many hours of discussions about life and librarianship, particularly about many of those feelings and ideas that are rarely given voice in academic libraries. Our one-on-one peer mentoring sessions in the workplace developed into a solid friendship outside the library where it was safe to admit to imposter syndrome, fear of failure, or fear of success. We practiced mindfulness and compassion together as we reminded each other to let go of our egos on a regular basis.

Both of us entered this profession to educate and mentor students, yet at the beginning of our careers we often felt cut off from our visions of service. The minutiae of academic life pulled us away from what we perceived at the time as "real connections" with students and faculty in the classroom and at the reference desk. As new librarians in an academic library, we identified our need for personal connections with our students and set a goal for ourselves to quantify a practice of engagement and service. This practice, we hoped, would prepare us to be more open to students, fellow faculty members, and our own interior dialogues, especially as we were challenged to merge with a slow-moving status quo that was often at odds with our "next new thing now" visions of librarianship.

In the years since creating the 360 Framework, we have come to understand that, as with all frameworks for practice, it is sometimes just plain hard to do on a regular basis. We have experienced the difficulty of finding time for contemplation or reflection during weeks filled with back-to-back meetings, planning sessions, instruction, and consultations with students. We know how a misplaced word with a colleague or a class session full of disinterested students can linger for days. In fact, we found that our practice of the 360 Framework ideals, especially in the beginning, sometimes opened us to more self-doubt or internal chatter.

That self-doubt that started in the midst of our practice was, thankfully, a catalyst for change. Knowing that we could think about and react to events in a different way was a powerful shift. We found that practicing the 360 Framework ideals did not change our inherent personalities, but it did transform our energy at work. We started viewing projects and interactions with a new awareness. Instead of fear, we found excitement; instead of drudgery, we found possibility. Working through that self-doubt, we continued to apply the 360 Framework as we knew that calm awareness, contemplativeness, and engaged communication would be the key drivers of success throughout our careers.

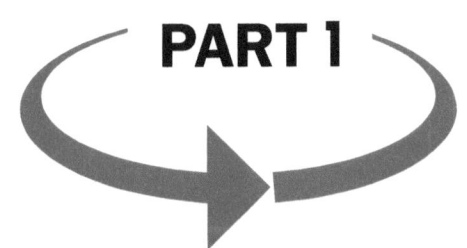

BUILDING A FRAMEWORK OF 360 LIBRARIAN IDEALS

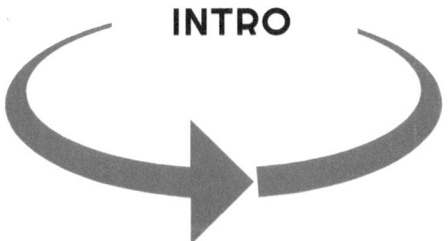

Introduction

Upon starting a new career or changing places of employment, there are often romantic notions of how this new journey will proceed. We hope that our coworkers will be kind, thoughtful, generous, and supportive. That we will make a difference while making meaningful connections with others. We want to be successful, effective, fulfilled, and appreciated. But what actually happens after we start a new career or a new job? The challenges. The trudging. The true, tough journey. We have to understand the official and unofficial mission of the organization, maneuver within the political landscape, mesh with colleagues' personalities and roles, and most importantly, learn how to do our job well. As we move through our careers, similar struggles may also be experienced when there is a change of management or mid-career burnout rears its ugly face. For many of these challenges, we are seldom given a guide on how to proceed. Without on-site mentors or a collaborative environment, it can feel as if we are walking in circles, lacking a compass that shows the way forward.

For both of us, this was exactly the case when we met as early-career librarians. We wished many times for a how-to guide to get us through interpersonal challenges, professional ups and downs, and moments of fear, doubt, and anxiety. This professional compass, we thought, would lead people just like us to the tools and practices needed to create their own authentic path. These tools would teach people how to respond to even the trickiest work situations with mindfulness, empathy, and compassion. Ultimately, we wanted a framework to show people like us how to sit back, reflect, refocus, and renew.

Building on concepts learned in multiple ACRL Immersion courses,[1] personal practices of mindfulness, and professional lives dedicated to service and intentionality, we created the 360 Framework to articulate our vision for practicing critically reflective librarianship with mindfulness and emotional intelligence at the forefront. Developing this five-step framework allowed us to become more purposeful in our daily interactions with students, faculty, and staff and created a way for us to signpost our efforts at authentic engagement. We curated or developed practical activities for our minds, bodies, and spirits to enhance and practice each step of the framework in order to become what we eventually defined as 360 librarians. The activities (*"Do the practice"*) were greatly expanded in this book to include the many questions we wish someone would have prompted us to reflect on years ago. To contextualize these practices, we've included semi-autobiographical case studies from our own work along with practical essays from librarians and educators in universities around the country.

The first area of the library to which we applied the Framework was the reference desk. In 2015, we contributed a chapter to *Teaching Reference Today: New Directions, Novel Approaches*, edited by Lisa A. Ellis.[2] *Teaching Reference Today*, which is dedicated to expanding the pedagogy of reference services, contains theoretical models and practical exercises for students, teachers, and library professionals. In our chapter, we introduced the 360 Framework as a way to strengthen one-on-one communication between reference librarians and students. As we extend the 360 Framework out from behind the reference desk to all areas of library work, the foundation of the practice remains the same.

The 360 Framework Ideals

An engaged library practice consists of continual give-and-take, careful assessment of others and oneself, and 360-degree, full-circle situational awareness. The five ideals a 360 Librarian should incorporate into their daily lives in order to provide a purposeful practice of service and engagement are:

1. Mindful Practice, or remaining in the moment in order to respond authentically and nonjudgmentally as situations arise.
2. Emotional Awareness, or noticing, assessing, and reacting accordingly to one's own and others' emotional states.
3. Engaged Communication, a combination of the awareness of nonverbal communication, the practice of deep listening, and deliberate two-way communication.
4. Empathetic Reflection and Action, a continuous state of learning about situational context and reacting in a considerate and appropriate manner.
5. Reassurance, the intentional act of bolstering one's own and others' confidence.

The 360 Framework ideals are built on three pillars of practice: mindfulness, emotional intelligence, and critical reflection. These skills allow us to acknowledge what is happening in the moment, observe our own and others' emotions, and calmly choose how to act or react in order to honor our commitment to our students and to the profession.

FIGURE 1.1.
360 Framework Ideals

Mindfulness

The practice of mindfulness, with its roots in Hinduism and Buddhism, has permeated modern professional and personal life. Today's secular practice of mindfulness is not about religion, nor does it conflict with any religious beliefs. It is about the art of conscious living.[3] Susan L. Smalley and Diana Winston define mindfulness as "the art of observing your physical, emotional, and mental experiences with deliberate, open and curious attention."[4] The act of careful attention results in mental clarity, improved professional performance, and greater emotional capacity for empathy and understanding. Mindfulness in the professional sphere is now practiced in business leadership, healthcare, education, and many other fields.

In the late 1970s, Jon Kabat-Zinn ushered mindfulness into the University of Massachusetts' psychology and neuroscience labs with the Mindfulness-Based Stress Reduction (MBSR) technique. Through a series of clinical trials, Kabat-Zinn and other researchers discovered that by purposefully acknowledging routine activities in a nonjudgmental way, patients undergoing treatment for a variety of illnesses were able to more effectively manage stress, pain, and illness and gain an awareness that led to a sense of agency, insight, and wisdom.[5] The MBSR technique has since been codified into in-person or online courses offered via UMass Medical School's Center for Mindfulness in Medicine, Healthcare, and Society or their certified teachers. We adhere to Kabat-Zinn's idea that you must examine yourself to gain a "greater awareness, clarity and acceptance of the present-moment reality" and that without this practice of single-pointed introspection people "fail to realize the… depth of our possibilities for growth.…"[6] It is this daily examination that we include in the 360 Librarian ideals and the growth that comes with a knowledge and acceptance of a present-moment reality that we seek.

We know that, as educator Deborah Schoeberlein David writes, mindfulness is not a panacea. It will not immediately make workplaces happier or difficult situations better. But mindfulness is a powerful tool to shift our perspective of and reaction to unavoidable or immutable situations in our lives.[7] Throughout the workday, we use mindfulness techniques to bring focus to our tasks and interactions. There are three main components to this practice of mindfulness outside the realm of meditation, writes psychologist Ellen Langer. For Langer, aspects of mindfulness are the creation of new categories in the mind, openness to new information, and awareness of more than one perspective. The ability to create new categories in the mind consciously turns practitioners away from mindless or habitual formations of thought and toward an attentive awareness of their surroundings and their ways of thinking. People who are open to new information are able to easily process stimulating new information and are mindful of the conversational cues that lead to effective communication. Awareness of more than one perspective encourages us to consider how others perceive our thoughts and actions because in everyday conversations there are potentially as many interpretations of what is said as there are participants in the conversation.[8] We have woven these three elements of mindfulness throughout the 360 Framework, especially during times of everyday practice.

In the education realm, many articles have listed the positive outcomes of educators who practice mindfulness in and out of the classroom. David writes that "mindfulness improves focus, increases responsiveness to students' needs, promotes emotional balance, supports stress management and stress reduction, supports healthy relationships, enhances climate and supports well-being."[9] And in a review of mindfulness in higher education, Dannielle Joy Davis concludes that mindfulness has positive effects on leadership in higher education which results in improved decision-making and organizational practices, improved morale, and increased empathy for others.[10] We have crafted the five 360 Librarian ideals to take advantage of these positive effects of mindfulness, as we believe these valuable qualities can and should translate into successful workplace interactions.

There are a few misconceptions surrounding mindfulness that we must resolve in order to build upon the practice as a pillar for the 360 Framework. First, mindfulness is often conflated with meditation and perceived as a time-consuming activity that is practiced on its own, like yoga. As part of our personal practices and in the 360 Framework, we understand that mindfulness extends to, and can be practiced in, everyday activities such as dressing, eating, walking, and even entering the workplace and listening to a coworker.[11] A second misconception is that mindfulness always requires single-minded deep concentration on a task, shutting out all other demands on one's attention. While some mindfulness practices train the mind in this manner, including several in this book, we both follow the teaching that mindfulness is a gentle reminder to return to the present when the mind wanders. This act releases thoughts that expend energy on the past and the future and grounds us in the present moment.[12]

Emotional Intelligence

Becoming adept at understanding others' emotions and managing one's own emotions through a variety of self-training methods is crucial to integrating the 360 Framework into your own practice. Our understanding of emotional intelligence comes largely from the work of Peter Salovey, John D. Mayer, and Daniel Goleman, who revolutionized the science and application of emotions.

In the 1980s, researchers began exploring the study of emotions as an independent field rather than as contributing factors in studies on social behavior or familial structures.[13] Salovey and Mayer contributed to the research of emotions with their groundbreaking research on emotional intelligence (EI), which they define as "the subset of social intelligence that involves the ability to monitor one's own and others' feelings and emotions, to discriminate among them and to use this information to guide one's thinking and actions."[14]

Salovey and Mayer's EI research was widely adopted in the fields of business and management, among others, with Goleman's publication of *Emotional Intelligence: Why it Can Matter More than IQ*. For Goleman, while technical acumen is important, emotional intelligence is as important as intellectual ability in the workplace, and the most successful employees are those who are able to manage their own and others' emotions.[15] Goleman outlines three intelligence domains that he maintains are the predictors of professional and personal success: IQ, practical intelligence, and emotional intelligence. IQ, or Intelligence Quotient, is perhaps the least indicative of success. When IQ test scores are examined in conjunction with work performance, according to Goleman, IQ predicts less than 25 percent of one's workplace achievement. With upwards of 75 percent of professional achievement left unexplained by one's IQ, it is necessary to examine other predictors of success.[16]

On-the-job expertise, or practical intelligence, is the second domain Goleman cites as a predictor of workplace achievement. While a reasonable understanding of the job coupled with hands-on experience offers a baseline for workplace competency, it does not provide the full picture to determine job performance success. For instance, job candidates who compete with peers for the same position typically possess similar IQs, as evidenced by the ability to pass entrance exams for college and obtain advanced degrees. The expertise that sets each of them apart is their practical intelligence, which is comprised of a combination of on-the-job training and sound judgment when dealing with customers and coworkers. This, Goleman explains, is "the real knowledge of how to do a job that only experience brings."[17]

The final domain that Goleman believes is the greatest contributor to success is emotional intelligence (EI). The EI framework is made up of five dimensions: self-awareness, self-regulation, motivation, empathy, and social skills. Within these five dimensions are a total of twenty-five competencies. While no one will be a master at all five dimensions, having strengths across these dimensions, coupled with an average to high IQ and practical intelligence, is the greatest predictor of professional success.[18]

Critical Reflection

We developed several of our 360 Framework ideals around the systematic thought processes of critical reflection in the works of John Dewey and Stephen Brookfield. In the early twentieth century, Dewey promoted the concept of reflective thinking in education as the act of questioning one's beliefs, reserving judgment, and investigating all facts and theories before coming to a well-reasoned conclusion. This, admits Dewey, is mentally uncomfortable as the act of suspending one's inclination to conclude one's thinking quickly results in a state of uneasiness that is sometimes difficult to bear. Dewey writes that problems or dilemmas, and the suspended judgment needed to attend to them, can be resolved via the logical, learned act of reflection. The educated and curious mind can be systematically trained in inductive and deductive reasoning, the rational and measured movement between the two being that which ultimately defines reflective thinking.[19] This is a crucial moment for learning in the classroom for our students and for us as reflective librarians who are willing to change and grow.

Critical reflection is an opportunity to make a fundamental change for an individual or an entire social or learning structure. In *Becoming a Critically Reflective Teacher*, Brookfield emphasizes that "[w]e reflect on our teaching so that we can create the conditions under which both teachers and students become aware of their own power of agency."[20] For Brookfield, critical reflection is a deep practice with the purpose of illuminating power dynamics and bringing to light hegemonic assumptions in the classroom. Brookfield offers four "lenses" with which to engage in critical reflection while teaching: "(1) our autobiographies as teachers and learners, (2) our students' eyes, (3) our colleagues' experiences, and (4) theoretical literature."[21]

In our original application of the 360 Framework to reference encounters, we focused primarily on Brookfield's first and second lenses. As we extended our practice to other areas of librarianship, we found that all of Brookfield's lenses can be helpful when incorporated into daily practice. We continue to encourage librarians to use the first lens, our autobiographies, to examine biases for or against learning or teaching methods, student or colleague attitudes, and new or existing ideas in the workplace. We interpret Brookfield's second lens, our students' eyes, in this context as becoming aware of the other person's perception in any given interpersonal encounter, with special emphasis given to encounters between faculty or staff and students. The third lens, our colleagues' experiences, turns the practice of 360 librarianship into a cooperative effort. As we've experienced by practicing the 360 ideals together, intention becomes mindful practice when inner dialogues are voiced and the experiences of many become shared lessons for all. The fourth lens, theoretical literature, reminds all of us to continue our own academic investigations for truth á la Dewey while we practice the 360 ideals.

Applying the 360 Framework

This book was written by academic librarians and, in its strictest sense, is focused on applications for and in academic libraries. This narrow focus allows us to bring our research, expertise, and personal reflections to bear on the 360 Librarian ideals. We have also been able to incorporate ideas and reflections of colleagues in college and research libraries in the 360 in Practice essays found throughout the book. Despite this book's focus on academic librarianship, we believe the 360 Framework ideals and the pillars of mindfulness, emotional intelligence, and critical reflection can and should be practiced by librarians and library staff in any professional situation at any time. The universal nature of the 360 Framework ideals also means they can be applied interdisciplinarily to the workplaces of archivists, curators, museum workers, and educators alike.

360 librarianship takes advantage of a flexible framework. It can be a personal and reflective practice, a team-oriented networked practice, or both. When practiced by multiple members of a team, the 360 Framework ideals can create a dynamic, integrated, and collaborative workplace. Awareness, communication, motivation, understanding, and synergy among team members will improve. On a personal level, practicing the 360 Framework will cultivate a new sense of self-awareness that can translate into improved leadership and conflict management skills.

The 360 Framework in action can have far-reaching impacts on your students, your workplace culture, and your entire organization. The combination of mindfulness, emotional intelligence, and critical reflection is a potent antidote to unhelpful interactions with colleagues as well as students, as it sets aside the fear of confrontation in the workplace and allows 360 Librarians to engage in positive practices to engender change. It is important to note, though, that some 360 practices are best completed in a safe and supportive environment. For example, honest one-to-one feedback among colleagues would be difficult in a competitive or aggressive workplace.

After reading *The 360 Librarian*, you may feel it is too overwhelming to practice everything all at once. Our first and continual reassurance is that 360 librarianship is a practice and, as such, we have ensured that the five steps of 360 librarianship complement and build on one another. You may choose to become comfortable or proficient in one step before adding another, or you may apply the Framework as a whole 360 practice continually until you become comfortable with all five steps at once.

You do not need any preparation to begin your 360 Librarian journey. An open, introspective mind and a positive attitude are helpful, as is a willingness to change. A new journal, a dedicated document on your laptop, or a private space online in which to record your reflections chapter by chapter may help you articulate nascent ideas and create connections among the five 360 Framework ideals. A truly confidential journal allows you to record your responses to the *Do the practice* prompts in each chapter with barebones honesty. This, in turn, promotes deep reflection and lasting transformation.

> *Do the practice*: This is an introductory practice that lays the groundwork for the framework to come. It offers you a chance to reflect on your strengths and challenges and articulate areas of opportunity before applying, reflecting on, and journaling specific 360 Framework practices.

Your day-to-day work
Reflect on a time where some of your most creative ideas or solutions came to mind. What emotions did you experience? What were you physically doing at the time? Now take a moment to reflect on a time when you felt overwhelmed with your workload and personal obligations. What emotions did you experience? Were solutions to your problems creative or were you putting out fires?

Your relationships at work
Reflect on your interpersonal relationships at work. Which relationships are positive and lift you up or "fill your bucket?" How do you contribute to filling other people's buckets? What emotions and feelings come with positive interactions? Which relationships feel toxic to you? Why do they feel toxic? Do you play a role in the toxicity of the relationship? What changes can you make to improve the relationship? What do you know about this person? What changes would you like to see from this person? Is either of you holding on to any past grievances that continue to fuel the toxicity? What changes would you like to see overall in this relationship?

Your culture at work
How would you describe the culture at your current workplace? Collegial and friendly? Businesslike? Politically fraught? If you could describe the perfect workplace, what would it include? How would your students act? How would colleagues interact with each other?

Your goals
What goals, dreams, and hopes would you have for your professional life? What support would you like to see in your dream work environment? How do you envision the role of the administration? What emotions would you experience? How would you be rewarded for success?

ENDNOTES

1. The ACRL (Association for College & Research Libraries) Information Literacy Immersion Programs are weeklong intensive sessions where participants actively engage with intellectual tools and practice techniques to elevate their professional skills. http://www.ala.org/acrl/immersion.

2. Carol A. Daul-Elhindi and Tammi M. Owens, "Reference 360: A Holistic Approach to Reference Instruction," in *Teaching Reference Today: New Directions, Novel Approaches,* ed. Lisa A. Ellis (Lanham: Rowman & Littlefield, 2016). Some aspects of the literature review and explanations of the five 360 Framework ideals have been adapted or reproduced from this earlier work, with permission from Rowman & Littlefield.
3. Jon Kabat-Zinn, *Wherever You Go, There You Are: Mindfulness Meditation in Everyday Life* (New York: Hyperion, 1994).
4. Susan Smalley and Diana Winston, "Is Mindfulness for You?" in *The Mindfulness Revolution: Leading Psychologists, Scientists, Artists, and Meditation Teachers on the Power of Mindfulness in Daily Life,* ed. Barry Boyce (Boston: Shambhala, 2011), 11.
5. Jon Kabat-Zinn, *Full Catastrophe Living: Using the Wisdom of Your Body and Mind to Face Stress, Pain, and Illness* (New York: Bantam Books, 2013). For a list of recent studies, see http://www.umassmed.edu/cfm/research/publications/.
6. Kabat-Zinn, *Wherever You Go,* 4.
7. Deborah Schoeberlein David, *Mindful Teaching and Teaching Mindfulness: A Guide for Anyone Who Teaches Anything* (Somerville, MA: Wisdom Publications, 2009).
8. Ellen J. Langer, *Mindfulness* (Boston: Da Capo Lifelong Books, 2014).
9. David, *Mindful Teaching,* 9.
10. Dannielle Joy Davis, "Mindfulness in Higher Education: Teaching, Learning, and Leadership," *International Journal of Religion & Spirituality in Society* 4, no. 3 (December 2014).
11. David, *Mindful Teaching.*
12. Smalley and Winston, "Is Mindfulness for You?"
13. Peter N. Stearns, "History of Emotions: Issues of Change and Impact," in *Handbook of Emotions,* 3rd ed., eds. Michael Lewis, Jeannette M. Haviland-Jones, and Lisa Feldman Barrett (New York: Guilford Press, 2008).
14. Peter Salovey and John D. Mayer, "Emotional Intelligence," *Imagination, Cognition and Personality* 9, no. 3 (March 1990): 189.
15. Daniel Goleman, *Emotional Intelligence: Why it Can Matter More than IQ* (New York: Bantam Books, 1997).
16. Daniel Goleman, *Working with Emotional Intelligence* (New York: Bantam Books, 2000).
17. Goleman, *Working with Emotional Intelligence,* 21.
18. Ibid.
19. John Dewey, *How We Think: A Restatement of the Relation of Reflective Thinking to the Educative Process* (Boston: D. C. Heath and Company, 1933).
20. Stephen Brookfield, *Becoming a Critically Reflective Teacher,* 1st ed. (San Francisco: Jossey-Bass, 1995), 217.
21. Brookfield, *Becoming a Critically Reflective Teacher,* 29.

CHAPTER 1
Mindful Practice

The first 360 Librarian ideal is Mindful Practice. Mindful Practice is the act of remaining in the moment in order to respond authentically and nonjudgmentally to situations that arise. This means that Mindful Practice, as is the case with other 360 Librarian ideals to come, consists of several different components. In this ideal, there are two main spheres of practice. The first, "the act of remaining in the moment," is related to attention at work and everyday life and is a fundamental quality of mindfulness. The second, the ability to "respond authentically and nonjudgmentally," is the reaction to the patterns that appear as a result of mindful attention to the thoughts and emotions of yourself and others.

Mindful Practice can be challenging in a fast-paced, multitasking profession like librarianship. Distractions come from many places: email, phone calls, meetings, emergencies at work or at home, even colleagues who stop by your office to chat. The most pernicious distraction for the 360 Librarian at the stage of Mindful Practice may be the internet. The ease of access to online resources means we can find, learn, or experience almost anything. A wealth of educational resources is available every second of every day, but this abundance can lead us to drift off to network with colleagues or catch up with friends on Facebook, shop for things on Amazon, or entertain ourselves on YouTube. Our purpose and intent when we go online may be work-related or educational, but a lack of focus and a wandering mind leads to hours lost pursuing online phantoms, even at work.

The constant distraction of multitasking or the pull of online tasks causes our attention to split. Divided attention creates a disconnect between what is happening in our lives and minds at that very moment and what our minds manufacture as other things that desperately need attention (email, Facebook, YouTube videos). This sudden disconnect can come between ourselves and our colleagues, ourselves and our work, and ourselves and that quiet place we need in order to be a kind and generous human being. Sometimes the disconnect results in uncomfortable feelings of unfulfillment, leaving us to wonder why we're misunderstood by the people around us or if we are working in jobs that aren't right for us. Sometimes that disconnected feeling just leaves us busy, stressed, and burned out in jobs we used to love.

Mindful Practice allows for conscious and purposeful actions and reactions that replace ingrained fear-based responses[1] and creates a culture that is marked by teamwork and genuine mutual support. Mindful Practice in itself will not eliminate all distractions, judgment, or bias, but it may relieve some of the stress that tends to narrow your field of focus to your own personal trials. It provides the space to empathetically engage, rather than react. The act of purposefully being in touch with coworkers and students opens up opportunities to fully engage with and learn from others while allowing for nonjudgmental discussion and creative inquiry.

This ideal is the action related to mindfulness, one of the pillars of the 360 Framework. Mindfulness is generally developed in two ways. The most well-known method is a focused-attention meditation practice. The practitioner focuses on their breath or an object, and as the mind starts to wander, they gently and without judgment bring their attention back to their breath or the object. This practice supports focused attention and mental well-being. The second method is an open awareness practice. The practitioner pays attention holistically, moment-by-moment, to events as they occur without trying to change or influence the outcome.[2] Labeling this ideal "Mindful Practice," instead of just mindfulness, reminds 360 Librarians that a series of small mindful moments throughout our workday can be as effective as a focused meditation practice. The act of moment-by-moment awareness practiced in the workplace may carry over into our personal lives as we strive to be continually mindful in our lives in general.

Structures and Relationships

Mindful Practice creates pathways in our brains to formulate deep relationships with ourselves and the world around us. Scientific studies prove these new pathways are quite literal, as mindfulness meditation training creates structural and functional changes in the brain. The structural effects of regular meditation result in thicker areas of the cerebral cortex related to attention and memory, along with a long list of newly developed reactive and processing behaviors in the mind and body. Functional changes of the brain in people who regularly meditate include increases in gamma brain waves that are associated with compassion and transcendence, or what neurobiological researcher Tobias Esch describes as a "dissolution of boundaries."[3]

Using Mindful Practice to cultivate healthy, robust relationships with others in personal and professional spheres can lead to better understanding and personal connection among one's peers,[4] naturally resulting in greater workplace satisfaction. An eighty-year longitudinal Harvard study has determined that the quality of personal relationships, more than any other characteristic, helps buffer people from moments of discontent. When the study began, empathy and attachment weren't on the researchers' list of considerations, but after several decades, researchers concluded that a strong network of personal relationships is highly associated with overall health and well-being.[5]

Jon Kabat-Zinn explains that mindfulness is a part of all our relationships, writing that mindfulness is about "relationality—how we are in relationship to everything, including our own minds and bodies, our thoughts and emotions, our past and what transpired to bring us, still breathing, into this moment—and how we can learn to live our way into every aspect of life with integrity, with kindness toward ourselves and others, and with wisdom."[6] While living mindfully takes practice and determination, Kabat-Zinn goes on to explain that "the cultivation of greater mindfulness also gives us new ways of working with what we find threatening, and of learning how to respond intelligently to such perceived threats rather than react automatically and trigger potentially unhealthy consequences."[7] Cultures around the world engage in practices such as prayer, meditation, Qigong, and yoga to establish the practice of nonjudgmental awareness in the moment. This focused awareness creates the transformational space to understand ourselves, which, in turn, builds a foundation for more meaningful connections with family, friends, coworkers, and students alike.[8]

Developing a Mindful Practice

The ability to focus attention or to stay in the moment nonjudgmentally can feel especially overwhelming when your mind feels cluttered and scattered. While a mindfulness meditation practice serves as a strong foundation for Mindful Practice, introducing simple awareness practices into daily living is an easy way to slow down the constant need to "do" and begin on a mindful path of reflection, contemplation, and "being." Jon Kabat-Zinn offers a few simple suggestions for mindful acts: practice short bursts of "non-doing" by placing attention onto your breath. While looking at people, suspend judgment and see them as they are rather than your perception of them that includes the images and thoughts of them entering your mind.[9] At work, try breaking free of the harmless stereotypes you may have laid on your colleagues. You might know some of the people at work as "the cataloguer who has three cats and likes goth music" or "our administrator who enjoys jellybeans and gardening" or "the student employee who hikes a lot." Your perception can be affected by these instant associations, and you may miss the opportunity to notice something new about a colleague and deepen that relationship. Likewise, associations, stereotypes, and assumptions can affect communication with those in your direct reporting structure. Negative associations are particularly sticky, as in the case of once poor-performing employees who are now excelling. Despite their current exemplary service, you might find yourself consciously or subconsciously seeking reasons to discount their work. You may attribute the reasons for their success to luck or fear of retribution instead of growth or talent. Resist this by remaining in the moment and actively cultivating nonjudgmental awareness.

Case study: Halfway through the university's spring semester, Coralie, a longtime library staff member who supervised a busy service desk, noticed that Ben, an otherwise kind and conscientious student employee, was transforming into what she reported as "a total slacker." Coralie felt Ben was "working the system" to cover or call out many of his Monday or Friday shifts, usually giving him a long weekend. He usually arranged last-minute coverage but sometimes called in sick and a few times did not show up at all. When he did come to work, he was often bleary-eyed and half-asleep in his chair. Coralie wanted to let Ben go before the end of the school year, but library administration asked her to help Ben get back to his high service level they noticed during Fall semester instead.

Remaining in the moment

While it is simple in theory to practice mindfulness, Kabat-Zinn reminds us that it is not easy. Our restless minds make it difficult to stay in a nonjudgmental, curious state and watch events without trying to change the outcome. Instead, the unsettled mind offers ideas on how to fix the situation, evaluates the various actions and reactions, and judges people, including ourselves, who are caught in the situation. This restless, unsettled state of being is most obvious when we work to calm the mind. During mindfulness training, physical sensations, inner speech, and various emotions bubble to the surface. Rest in the fact that this is normal and bound to happen. Allow these sensations, thoughts, and emotions to rise. Without judging, notice what comes to the surface. Allow the practice to shed light on areas of your life where you may be out of touch.[10] The Mindful Practice of paying attention to your breath can serve as the basis for all further Mindful Practice exercises associated with workplace interactions.

> *Do the practice:* One common mindfulness breathing exercise is a practice called breath counting, which we have adapted here for use in the workplace.
>
> Choose something that happens regularly during your workday. At work, it could be the chime of your email, sit-

ting back down in your chair, or picking up a book to catalog. Take a deep breath and exhale through your nose. Feel the breath on your face. Next, take a more measured breath, and again breathe out through your nose. Feel the tiny exhale under your nostrils. Inhale and exhale in a natural way. Count each exhale, up to five, before you answer your email, turn back to your work, or catalog the book.

This breathing practice can also be a centering or calming device. When you feel yourself getting distracted, tired, or emotional, return to your breath. The breath is a reminder of the fleeting nature of thoughts and feelings. Returning to the anchor of the breath may eventually become a natural response during stressful situations.

Eventually, you may want to continue this practice at home. In everyday life, some people choose reminders like a red traffic light or the clock chiming the hour. Or you may want to begin this meditation practice without a cue. In any case, continue counting your breaths, or just breathe when you are faced with your reminder. Notice your breath standing in line, or waiting at a stoplight, or listening to the phone ring. You may want to count to five, or three, or seven, but choose a number that is easy for you to remember. If your mind wanders and you find yourself counting past your chosen number, gently bring your mind back to start over with the first breath.

Breath counting can be a fraught proposition for some of us. At the beginning of one phase of intensive meditation practice, Tammi would swear she couldn't remember how to breathe. To her, it felt like she spent hours sitting and panting while others around her seemed untroubled by simple breathing. Sometimes, it's not just tricks of the mind. Medical conditions such as asthma or anxiety can leave us literally breathless. If that is the case for you, it is important to acknowledge this and turn to another form of Mindful Practice.[11] Continuing to fight against your own breath and finding tightness and anxiety instead of attention and clarity is not at all the intention of this ideal. You may consider focusing your attention instead on the sensation of your feet on the floor, the sensation in your hands, or the feeling of your weight on the chair as alternatives to focused breathing.[12]

Many 360 Librarians may find strength and ease in Mindful Practice by paying closer attention to both ordinary and extraordinary moments throughout the day. It's a common practice to run into the office at eight o'clock each morning thinking of nothing but the meetings and projects and timelines for the day to come. We rush in, sit down at our desk, turn on the computer, dive into email, and time flies by. All of a sudden, it's time to go home and we leave wondering what we did all day and if we accomplished anything we intended to at the beginning of the day. Mindful Practice in the workplace disrupts this process, if only for a few minutes, and replaces it with brief moments of awareness. Mindful Practice to reconnect the mind and body can happen anywhere: at your desk, over lunch, even walking across campus. The only preparation needed for an ordinary moment of practice is to prepare the mind by *letting go of* the mind. Drop the problems of the present and the expectations of the future and just do the practice.

> *Do the practice:* One common Zen teaching to cultivate mindfulness is mindful eating. Thich Nhat Hanh asks us, while eating, to consider where the food came from. While slowly taking a bite and chewing, feel the texture, notice the taste and smell, feel the food particles as they are swallowed and make their way to your stomach. Once you have completed your meal, consider the impact of your food choices on you, your surroundings, and your environment.[13]

> *Do the practice:* Thich Nhat Hanh counsels that a moving mindful practice may be more conducive than a passive mindful practice when we are experiencing pent up anxious energy.[14] Instead of ruminating or becoming anxious, walk mindfully through the library or across campus. As you move, notice the physical sensations in your feet and legs, raise your head to take in the visual cues that surround you, and notice, without judgment, the emotions that arise as you pass an acquaintance. Zen walking meditation typically consists of extremely slow, purposeful movements, but as a daily practice in the workplace, don't walk fast or slow. Just walk. You may have a destination in mind, but keep your thoughts from your desk or your destination. See what comes before you. Try not to make up stories or let what you see influence your mind. If you see something out of the ordinary, stop to investigate. Don't take a picture. Instead, watch and wonder. Enjoy that very moment.

> *Do the practice:* Turn your attention toward the visual arts by creating a mindful word or image in your 360 Journal. Acquire a broad-tipped pen or brush and experiment with cal-

ligraphic lines or letters. Using your breath as a focal point, mindfully follow the strokes of the pen or brush as it crosses the page. Write a word or phrase that inspires or calms you. Or, create a mindful image or "zendoodle," also known as Zentangle. The abstract, repetitive patterns of a zendoodle offer another outlet for your focused attention. Relax as you create your designs. Even if you don't consider yourself artistic, understand that in both of these creative practices there are no mistakes and so you cannot do it wrong. Release any judgmental inner critics and celebrate your mindful art.

Case study, continued: One hectic day, Coralie rushed into work as usual. Ben was at the service desk, listless, at a workstation well out of student view. Preoccupied with the morning antics of her own school-age children and still in "hurry-up" mode, Coralie spoke more harshly than usual as she admonished Ben about his attitude and what she called his "hiding place." Ben moved to a more central computer but was more sullen than ever and finished out his shift in silence. Later that day, Coralie walked across campus and back during her lunch hour. She spent twenty minutes walking, breathing, and observing the flow of campus life during her walk. When she came back to her desk, she felt more grounded. Now that she had time to step out of her parenting role, she realized that she was bringing her preconceived notions of young adult "antics" and student employee attitudes into her supervisory decisions about Ben's behavior. Instead of looking for more reasons to write Ben up and dismiss him, Coralie decided to ask Ben to come in for a meeting.

Becoming an authentic communicator through nonjudgmental awareness

Mindful Practice opens the mind to authentic communication. This process begins from within, as a deeper awareness of the beliefs and assumptions that propel you through daily life comes through the practice of mindful critical reflection. Mindfully noticing and existing with your beliefs and assumptions, without judgment, creates an awareness of the dissonance between your thoughts and beliefs and your words and actions. Noticing this dissonance and making intentional changes to align the things you say and do with your core beliefs is how the authentic self naturally evolves.[15]

Another path to authentic communication is by peeling away your ego and turning away from the need to be "right." This is a hard practice. Reflecting on our mistakes, accepting critical feedback, and sharing this feedback with others at the workplace can be an uncomfortable experience that can leave any human feeling defensive, and it may be doubly so for people in a service profession like librarianship. Push against defensiveness with honest self-reflection and nonjudgmental awareness. This practice opens space in your thoughts for self-compassion and self-improvement, the cultivation of which begets honest, empathetic, and emotionally intelligent relationships with others.

Nonjudgmental awareness is the practice of sitting with your thoughts and reacting to situations without assessing whether they are good or bad, attractive or repulsive, pleasant or unpleasant. Value judgments shroud experiences with a veil of our own past experiences and assumptions about correct behavior. It's easy to make snap judgments when working with coworkers and students, rather than stepping back and viewing the situation with curiosity. The mind can quickly travel from "this student is violating our computer use policy" to "why can't they just follow the rules?" and worse. Developing mindful awareness creates the space to reflect on the thoughts and emotions that arise when interacting with social partners rather than reacting with exasperation and frustration.[16] Practicing nonjudgmental awareness doesn't mean there is a total absence of judgment or a consistent tendency to capitulate. Instead, nonjudgmental awareness hones the ability to "cultivate discernment" and focus on the situation at hand.[17]

> *Do the practice:* As part of an online Mindfulness-Based Stress Reduction video, Jon Kabat-Zinn offers this practice to expand your nonjudgmental awareness: When you are faced with a difficult situation, listen with curiosity as the facts and circumstances unfold. Judgmental thoughts will undoubtedly arise. Notice them and let them go, rather than interjecting biased thoughts. This process creates the opportunity to view the interaction from a non-biased perspective and understand the reasoning behind your communication partners thoughts and motives. In addition, you may want to ask clarifying questions such as "Tell me more about…", "How did you feel when…", "What outcome would you like to see?"[18] Write down these interactions, including the scenario, the questions you asked, and the answers you received in your 360 Journal.

> *Do the practice:* With large parts of the day spent sitting in offices, meetings, and at lunch, this Desk Chair Meditation offers an opportunity to incorporate mindful practice to ground oneself before a meeting or recharge after a stressful encounter.[19]

- Begin by bringing your attention to the sensations of your breath.
- When you're ready, direct your attention to the soles of your feet, opening your mind to whatever sensations are there to be noticed. Perhaps you are noticing the pressure on the soles of your feet as the weight of your legs rests on them. Perhaps the soles of your feet feel warm or cool.
- Just notice. No need to judge or engage in discursive thinking. If your mind is pulled away or wanders, redirect your attention, firmly and gently.
- Move your attention next to the tops of your feet, ankles, lower legs, knees, and so forth. Gradually scan through your body, noticing sensations, noticing discomfort, and noticing areas of your body where you detect an absence of sensations. You simply don't notice any sensations in your shoulders right now, for example. No need to search for sensations; just keep scanning through your body, taking your time and being open to what is here.

As you practice nonjudgmental awareness, you will eventually notice that your own values, beliefs, assumptions, or personal history no longer controls your thoughts, actions, and reactions. Instead, you can respond with calm, sincere, resonant action.

Case study, continued: To make sure she completely understood Ben's situation before confronting him on his poor performance, Coralie asked Ben to meet with her later that afternoon. Coralie was surprised that Ben arrived at that meeting refreshed and more coherent than he usually was at work. Remembering the clarity that came with her lunchtime walk, Coralie gently shelved her surprise and instead just asked Ben about his day and his semester. Ben started telling Coralie how tough things had been for him in the last few months. A farm kid from a small town several hours from the university, Ben had often been called back to help his family with early-morning chores or long weekends of work. He was also taking classes for which he ended up reading long into the night. When Ben was through explaining his recent challenges, Coralie told him how pleased everyone in the library was with his fall semester service and asked if he thought he could attain that service level again and, if so, how he would go about doing that. Ben asked if he could officially trade shifts with his friend who worked over the dinner hour and pledged to check with Coralie first before committing to any more long weekends at the family farm.

Integrating Mindful Practice

Mindful Practice can begin from the moment you awaken. Turn off the morning autopilot and pay attention to the moments of your life as they unfold, writes Deborah Schoeberlein David. It is this conscious awareness and silent acknowledgment of doing things like waking up, showering, brushing your teeth, engaging with the barista, and greeting a colleague that transforms mindless motions into an experiential activity.[20] For example, for many people, their shower is either an extension of their slumber or it's a time to plan out their day. Instead, try focusing your attention on the act of showering. How does it feel to wash your hair? If you typically stand half-asleep in the shower, can you identify the moment when you turn from "sleepy" to "awake"?

After you consciously attend to your day, David encourages the act of setting an intention for the day. This requires a dutiful concentration to that intention regardless of your schedule throughout the day. For example, you might set an intention like: "Today, I will aspire to move through my day without judging myself or my students." As the day unfolds, you will notice moments of successfully (or not-so-successfully) suspending judgment and accepting moments as they happen. If moments of judgment arise, take note, then consciously decide to suspend that judgment. Over time, as you practice your intention of suspending judgment, you will be able to notice and acknowledge longer spans of judgment-free moments than before.[21] Intention-setting works well for any repetitive thoughts or emotions you wish to suspend or actions you wish to encourage in yourself or others.

Anyone in any job role can practice this ideal in the workplace. People in leadership roles, though, may have an extra incentive to train their mind to focus attention and remain in the moment nonjudgmentally. Leaders who engage in Mindful Practice have an opportunity to change their own professional trajectories, influence the behavior and relationships of the employees they supervise, and alter the workplace culture.[22] Mindful leaders express a palpable calm, confident, nonjudgmental energy. In the presence of a mindful leader, there is a feeling that you are receiving their full attention, you are important, and you are valued.

Janice R. Marturano defines a mindful leader as one who not only provides the space or "breathing room" to be present but also one who "embodies leadership presence by cultivating focus, clarity, creativity, and compassion in the service of others."[23] *Focus* is perhaps one of the most difficult aspects, as research shows that we are focused and present just 53 percent of the time.[24] Distraction leads to not only a lack of productivity but also results in a disconnect between you and your colleagues when your mind wanders during a conversation.[25] Do the breath counting practice or read the Mindful Practice section in the 360 Librarian Practice in Leadership chapter to integrate focus into your leadership role.

Clarity is the ability to take a step back and pause the internal thoughts and judgments providing space to see the situation clearly.[26] While it seems counterintuitive to slow down during a fast-paced busy workday, creating the space to challenge our assumptions provides the opportunity to move away from rigid, fixed beliefs and reactions and respond with compassion and fluidity. Clarity tends to naturally appear more frequently as your Mindful Practice deepens.

Creativity happens when the mind has an opportunity to wander away from a to-do list or personal concerns and wander toward self-reflection, envisioning solutions, or just pondering life.[27] We champion breath counting or mindful awareness as an avenue for this wandering, but moments of unstructured thinking or brainstorming are appropriate for creative mindfulness as well. Marturano writes that when the mind engages in a break from analytical thinking—for example, just upon waking up, while enjoying a cup of tea, on a run or a walk—it provides the space for incubating new ideas.[28]

Compassion, a critical characteristic for mindful leaders, reaches beyond pity or sympathy for another person's misfortunes and recognizes that we are all interconnected within humanity.[29] Developing compassion for others begins with cultivating self-compassion. A conscious effort to suspend negative self-talk and replace it with kindness leads to an awareness of how we may actually be creating suffering.[30] If you find the practice of everyday compassion or empathy (for others or for yourself) difficult, complete the practices in chapter 4, Empathetic Reflection and Action.

When 360 Librarians adopt a Mindful Practice, they allow themselves space to teach, mentor, and lead with calm and focused intention. Beginning with the breath and expanding into moments throughout the workday, Mindful Practice is a conduit for kindness, empathy, and compassion. Relationships built with Mindful Practice, whether brief or long-term, can have a resonance that nurtures creative ideas and promotes innovative experimentation throughout the library.

ENDNOTES

1. Jon Kabat-Zinn, *Full Catastrophe Living: Using the Wisdom of Your Body and Mind to Face Stress, Pain, and Illness* (New York: Bantam Books, 2013).
2. Steven S. Parkin, Matthew S. Jarman, and Robin R. Vallacher, "On Being Mindful: What Do People Think They're Doing?," *Social and Personality Psychology Compass* 9, no. 1 (January 1, 2015), https://doi.org/10.1111/spc3.12156.
3. Tobias Esch, "The Neurobiology of Meditation and Mindfulness," in *Meditation— Neuroscientific Approaches and Philosophical Implications: Studies in Neuroscience*

      Consciousness and Spirituality, eds. Stefan Schmidt and Harald Walach (Cham: Springer, 2014), https://doi.org/10.1007/978-3-319-01634-4_9, 158–59.
4. Kirk Warren Brown, Richard M. Ryan, and J. David Creswell, "Mindfulness: Theoretical Foundations and Evidence for its Salutary Effects," *Psychological Inquiry* 18, no. 4 (October 2007), https://doi.org/10.1080/10478400701598298.
5. Liz Mineo, "Good Genes are Nice, but Joy is Better," *Harvard Gazette*, April 11, 2017, http://news.harvard.edu/gazette/story/2017/04/over-nearly-80-years-harvard-study-has-been-showing-how-to-live-a-healthy-and-happy-life/.
6. Kabat-Zinn, *Full Catastrophe Living*, xxxvii.
7. Ibid., xxxviii.
8. Daniel J. Siegel, *The Mindful Brain: Reflection and Attunement in the Cultivation of Well-Being*, 1st ed. (New York: W. W. Norton, 2007).
9. Jon Kabat-Zinn, *Wherever You Go, There You Are: Mindfulness Meditation in Everyday Life* (New York: Hyperion, 1994).
10. Kabat-Zinn, *Wherever You Go*.
11. Thich Nhat Hanh and Katherine Weare, *Happy Teachers Change the World: A Guide for Cultivating Mindfulness in Education* (Berkeley, CA: Parallax Press, 2017).
12. Hanh and Weare, *Happy Teachers*.
13. Ibid.
14. Ibid.
15. Barbara Larrivee, *Authentic Classroom Management: Creating a Learning Community and Building Reflective Practice* (Upper Saddle River, NJ: Pearson, 2009).
16. Patricia Jennings, *Mindfulness for Teachers: Simple Skills for Peace and Productivity in the Classroom* (New York: W. W. Norton & Company, 2015).
17. Jon Kabat-Zinn, "The Attitude of Non-Judging," Mindfulness Training Online MBSR, accessed August 20, 2017, https://www.youtube.com/watch?v=OwVkxcw1eZE.
18. Kabat-Zinn, "The Attitude of Non-Judging."
19. Janice Marturano, *Finding the Space to Lead: A Practical Guide to Mindful Leadership* (New York: Bloomsbury Press, 2014); "Desk Chair Meditation," excerpted from *Finding the Space to Lead: A Practical Guide to Mindful Leadership* (page 51) by Janice Marturano. Find the entire guided meditation at https://instituteformindfulleadership.org/guided-meditation-desk-chair-meditation/. Marturano is the Institute Director for the Institute for Mindful Leadership (https://instituteformindfulleadership.org/), used with permission.
20. Deborah Schoeberlein David, *Mindful Teaching and Teaching Mindfulness: A Guide for Anyone Who Teaches Anything* (Somerville, MA: Wisdom Publications, 2009).
21. David, *Mindful Teaching*.
22. Richard Moniz et al., *The Mindful Librarian: Connecting the Practice of Mindfulness to Librarianship* (Waltham, MA: Chandos Publishing, 2016).
23. Janice Marturano, *Finding the Space*, 11.
24. Matthew A. Killingsworth and Daniel T. Gilbert, "A Wandering Mind Is an Unhappy Mind," *Science* 330, no. 6006 (November 2010).
25. Marturano, *Finding the Space*.
26. Ibid.

27. Daniel Goleman, *Focus: The Hidden Driver of Excellence,* 1st ed. (New York: Harper, 2013).
28. Marturano, *Finding the Space.*
29. Ibid.
30. Shauna L. Shapiro and Linda E. Carlson, *The Art and Science of Mindfulness: Integrating Mindfulness into Psychology and the Helping Professions* (Washington, DC: American Psychological Association, 2009).

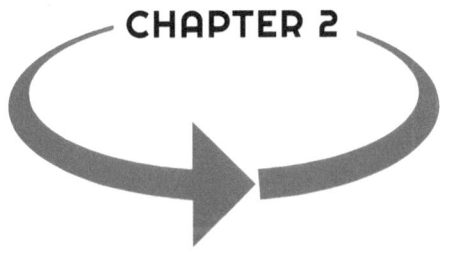

CHAPTER 2

Emotional Awareness

Emotional Awareness, the second 360 Librarian ideal, is the act of noticing, assessing, and reacting accordingly to one's own and others' emotions in order to generate a calm, reassuring, and overall positive experience regardless of the context of the interaction. Emotionally aware interactions are not just public-facing at the library; in fact, Emotional Awareness is a sensibility upon which all remaining ideals are practiced throughout the organization. For a 360 Librarian, Emotional Awareness is the underlying component for improving communication, strengthening relationships, increasing empathy, and providing excellent service.

The Emotional Awareness ideal is based on Salovey, Mayer, and Goleman's Emotional Intelligence theories discussed in the introduction, but there is an active element to this ideal that is wrapped in the actions of the other ideals. Intellectual ability and technical acumen are important and required to perform well in any given occupation, but it is emotionally intelligent values such as empathy, initiative, adaptability, leadership, ability to work as a team, and persuasiveness that sets coworkers apart when it comes to success in the workplace.[1] Emotional Awareness is the ability to blend the values of emotional intelligence with mindfulness and a willingness to critically engage, reflect, and act. This creates a culture of trust, compassion, creativity, resilience, and authentic connection within the workplace.

The intended outcome of a daily Emotional Awareness practice is the mindful application of one's own emotions in order to specifically *positively* affect any interaction, including self-talk. Practicing the intention for positive interactions and outcomes are building blocks for other parts of the 360 Framework which, when combined, can change an institution's culture. This is especially true for situations which at face value seem laden with negative emotion. For instance, practicing Emotional Awareness individually or as a team can make it easier to mindfully unpack a tricky problem, to embrace failure, or begin a difficult conversation with an unhappy or intractable colleague.

To be adept at the ideal of Emotional Awareness, librarians should recognize emotions in themselves and others and work to create a positive workplace experience. Emotional Awareness requires strengthening emotional intelligence through a mindful approach to assess one's own and others' emotions and to acknowledge how feelings and emotions are contributing to verbal and nonverbal behavior.[2] Perhaps you have been witness to a department meeting where intense workplace emotions caused colleagues to erupt or walk out of the meeting derailing a project, or alternatively experienced working with a task force where collegiality was the norm and emotions such as joy, inspiration, and pride flowed following the completion of the task. Even small moments of rudeness have been shown to be contagious in the workplace and may lead to more serious negative behavior.[3] The ability to de-escalate an uncomfortable confrontation requires the emotional self-control to stay calm under pressure, the empathy to understand the nonverbal emotional displays, and the influence to find common ground with which to calm and reassure others that they are being heard.

Strong emotions of any kind are valuable to Emotional Awareness. Be mindful of all emotions and pay special attention to anger and outrage emanating from yourself or others. Anger and outrage and their internalized cousins, disappointment and fear, are indications of inequality, ineffectiveness, or dysfunction. It is not helpful to react while in the midst of negative emotions, but use your anger and outrage or other strong feelings as a motivation to identify and address injustice in your workplace.

The Science and Psychology of Emotion

Prior to Peter Salovey and John D. Mayer's seminal 1990 work on emotional intelligence, many scholars held that emotions and intelligence were contradictory and emotions were considered "disorganized interruptions of mental activity."[4] Decades of research since has established that the ability or inability to regulate emotions is much more than a mere interruption in our minds. Emotional regulation can have ramifications in many areas of our lives, writes Maya Tamir. It is a goal-oriented act motivated by a desire to change one's "physiology, cognition, motivation, behavior or their social environment."[5] Goleman echoes this sentiment as he outlines the characteristics that emotionally aware people possess. He notes that individuals skilled in emotional awareness "naturally use their emotional radar to sense how others are reacting, and they fine-tune their own response to push the interaction in the best direction."[6]

Scientific studies show the existence of an emotional link between conversational partners, even if they are strangers.[7] For example, when meeting someone for the first time, if the conversation is going well, new acquaintances begin to mirror each other's behaviors and speech patterns. Goleman, Boyatzis, and McKee note the most that contagious emotions are at each end of the spectrum: cheerfulness, warmth, rudeness, and grumpiness.[8] Carol witnessed this contagion effect at an International House of Pancakes in Wisconsin Dells, Wisconsin. The restaurant's manager, seeing the long and slightly agitated line of families waiting for tables on Mother's Day, cracked jokes and sang each family's name when their table was ready to keep the mood light—and it worked. When a customer complimented him on his emotionally aware interpersonal skills, he replied, "If I don't keep you happy here, nothing we do in the dining room will satisfy you." As an emotional leader, he was able to combat any swell of negative emotion in the entire waiting area with his own positive communication style.

Knowing about the emotional link and transmission between conversational partners may make it easier to recognize and identify the source of emotions in the workplace and plan for calm and connected interactions, even with the general public. When practicing Emotional Awareness, try to adopt the role of the emotional leader during interactions and expressively transmit calm positive feelings. Goleman, Boyatzis, and McKee remind us that negative emotions, if left unchecked, can have a significant effect on students and colleagues. Anxiety and distress can have a negative impact on cognitive capabilities, as these feelings tend to reduce one's ability to be empathetic, diminish social skills, and ultimately result in an inability to demonstrate emotional intelligence.[9]

The ability to regulate emotions requires more than an intellectual understanding that these skills will be beneficial in all aspects of life. It requires a procedural understanding of how to put these skills and techniques into action. The ability to employ the emotional awareness skills necessary for lasting change "requires the retooling of ingrained habits of thought, feeling and behavior."[10] Fortunately, Emotional Awareness skills such as empathy, social awareness, and self-awareness can be heightened throughout life and often improve with maturity.[11]

Practicing Emotional Awareness

The practice of Emotional Awareness within the 360 Framework is a steady, internal process. It is deeply enmeshed with the other internal practices of Mindful Practice and Empathetic Reflection and Action and complements the more externally focused ideals of Engaged Communication and Reassurance. Emotional Awareness continually retrains the brain and body to mark the decision points of noticing, assessing, and reacting to emotions. Like any other physical training, the Emotional Awareness "muscle" strengthens with practice until it becomes an intuitive part of communication.

Strengthening the Emotional Awareness muscle to the point of second nature is a valuable protection against the draining emotional labor of librarianship. Emotional Awareness trains you to mindfully and thoughtfully view and understand emotions without becoming ensnared by them. The non-attachment exercises below cork the drain of our work, in a sense. In the practice of Emotional Awareness, other people's emotions are important and valuable to communication, but you will not need to internalize the words, actions, and feelings of other people. You can be a positive force without carrying wounds.

Noticing emotions

Setting the emotional tone or adjusting to others' emotions during an interaction cannot be accomplished without the ability to recognize and regulate one's own emotions. Bolstering Emotional Awareness, then, begins with the admittedly difficult task of becoming self-aware. Self-awareness, explains Travis Bradberry, is more than recognizing arising emotions and their ripple effects, although we mark that recognition of emotions is a valuable talent in its own right.[12] Self-awareness is a sometimes uncomfortable journey of self-discovery to understand personal values, strengths, and limitations as well as intrinsic and extrinsic motivators by leaning into and unpacking moments of emotional discomfort. Much of the time, uneasy emotional states trigger elaborate self-talk that includes deflection onto others to explain the uncomfortable situation. With self-awareness, the experience of emotional discomfort allows for the opportunity to understand internal triggers that surround the uncomfortable feelings. This, in turn, motivates us to recognize where we can make changes to avoid feelings of discontentment that accompany avoidance behavior.[13] Psychologist Anna Maravelas suggests that two self-defeating habits of smart people are to blame others or to blame themselves. Maravelas encourages those "smart people" to, instead of falling into blame, be curious and ask questions to clarify assumptions to find out more about the situation.[14]

> *Do the practice:* Begin noticing your own emotions by mindfully analyzing pleasant and unpleasant daily encounters. What topics or experiences make you elated, proud,

and interested, and which make you angry, defensive, or retreat? Consider what emotions you experience when you disagree with a colleague, when a demanding student approaches the desk, or when you propose an innovative idea that is met with resistance. Document the emotions and feelings, as well as the physical sensations that arise in your 360 Journal. Eventually, after some time (one day, one week, or one month), you will analyze the patterns you see in the effort to become more self-aware. But for now, just practice mindfully noticing and documenting your emotions as they arise.

Noticing others' emotions springs from self-awareness. So often our own emotions are so loud or muddled in our minds that we can't settle our attention onto someone else. Noticing others' emotions is a type of mindful engagement with another person, actively reflecting on their words and other modes of communication. It is *concentrated listening* to words, conversational cues, and body language. Only after this concentrated listening can you place everything in situational context, assess the emotions, and react. For those of us with short attention spans, those who become easily enthusiastic about new ideas and tend to interrupt, or those who tend toward pessimistic reactions, concentrated listening is a difficult and very active practice. It involves setting aside the ego, being willing to put other people first, and trusting that you will get time to speak and express your own ideas.

Do the practice: Notice others' emotions by first clearing your own emotional reaction to pleasant and unpleasant daily encounters. While your own emotions are important, in the workplace it is often more important to react to interactions calmly and as positively as possible, which may mean acknowledging but not acting on your own feelings at first. Instead, take the opportunity to investigate the spoken and unspoken communication of the other person. Using the practice of Engaged Communication, can you identify physical "tells" of someone's mood? What words are they using? Are they positive or negative words? Do their words match their body language? Think about the power relation of you and your communication partner. Are you equals at work? Who is "in charge" in this particular exchange? Keep in mind that, even if you are the supervisor, the other person may be speaking from a position of power if they are speaking about their expertise or personal experience. Conversely, you may find that they manifest emotions of powerlessness or lack of control despite their expertise within the conversation. Document these emotions and feelings in a journal entry.

In some difficult situations or toxic workplaces, the thought of approaching any interaction without emotional armor may seem unimaginable. This is exactly the time when you need to fall back on self-awareness to understand and become comfortable with your feelings of discomfort. Someone else's emotional reaction to any situation does not have to create any sort of reaction on your part. A highly charged or toxic workplace does leave you with more emotional labor to do, though, as you must quickly identify, process, and let go of emotions in order to just do your job. For difficult situations or toxic workplaces, use a journal entry to document negative interactions in detail.

Case study: One evening, just as the clock was about to strike 9 p.m., Eugene was packing up his papers and computer and getting ready to close the reference desk. A student approached. She said she needed some articles for a speech she had to give the next day but was unable to find anything. Although Eugene was looking forward to going home and disappointed that this extra reference encounter would prevent him from leaving on time, he reflected that student needs and superior customer service come before his schedule. Five or ten minutes with this student might be an important part of their learning history. Eugene noticed the student's trembling hands and breathless, rushed speech patterns. He could have sent the student away as the reference desk was closed for the day, but this student clearly needed help.

Assessing emotions

The assessment of emotions is a liminal state. In the whole practice of Emotional Awareness, assessing is the quick half-step of "What is this?" between "I've noticed" and "I'll do." It is also fragile and fallible in practice. Especially in the workplace, where assessing and acting upon emotions is often an atypical process, this step is most fruitful when it is motivated by curiosity and kindness instead of blame, shame, or fear. It should also be accompanied by a healthy dose of skepticism in your own abilities. You are not right or wrong in your assessment of your own or someone else's emotions; in this context, assessment is not a value judgment. It is the mechanism for data collection during the practice of Emotional Awareness.

Self-assessment of emotions is an inward-looking, honest appraisal of how and why you react to people or situations. During the practice of Emotional Awareness, you can step as far into or away from self-awareness as you prefer. Goleman positions self-assessment as a practice of "learning from experience" and an opportunity to be "open to candid feedback, new perspectives, continuous learning, and self-development,"[15] but it does not necessarily have to be that deep-seated. For this ideal, this is the time to link events or interactions to feelings and actions. Depending on your personal journey and the questions you ask yourself, you may decide to extend your self-awareness and reflect on your values, strengths, limitations, and motivations.

> *Do the practice:* Look back at your journal with special attention to the moments when you noticed your own emotions. Do similar emotions arise during similar interactions, like nervousness during meetings or awkwardness in the breakroom? Do you feel most fulfilled in the classroom or at peace when giving tours of your building? When you go into these situations, understand that you may feel these emotions again. Before entering these situations, think about why you tend to associate these feelings with these events and decide whether or not you would like to change the emotions or the outcome of the events. Think about how others may have perceived the same interaction. Do you think they felt the same as you did? How was your internal state different from or the same as your external state?

Assessing others' emotions takes patience to perceive and contextualize the situation without immediate judgment. Classical research on emotion recognition by researchers such as Paul Ekman state that recognition of the facial expression of the six basic emotions (happiness, sadness, anger, fear, disgust, and surprise) are universally recognized and understood around the world, but Lisa Feldman Barrett's research presents the opposite view: that emotions are constructed. Barrett writes that it is impossible to assess another person's emotions directly using external cues and your understanding of the interaction. Instead, external emotional cues are always filtered through your perception, which can be altered by your own life experiences, your emotions, or your understanding of the situation. Barrett contends that "to improve at emotion perception, we must all give up the fiction that we know how other people feel."[16]

Do the practice: With judgment suspended, look through your notes on your communication partners' emotions. Could these emotions be a result of their personal convictions? Being careful not to stereotype, ask yourself if their (or your) values or ethics are being challenged. Consider the perspective of your communication partner. Are there challenges your communication partner may be dealing with, like hunger, fatigue, or a physical or emotional diagnosis? How would you respond to this situation if you were in their place? Consider your own perspective. Are you reacting to the situation? How are your emotional reactions impacting those around you?

With this collected data, the next step is to examine the patterns you notice. Diligently noticing and analyzing emotional reactions allows you to create what Joan Giesecke calls an "internal database of your approach to emotional encounters."[17] An awareness of situations that make you react negatively, along with an understanding of how your reactions impact others, may create an opportunity for you to take a breath and gain control. It provides the space to be curious and clarify assumptions, as Maravelas suggests. This mindful approach to emotional awareness will intuitively lead you to respond differently the next time you are confronted with a similar scenario.[18] A word about empathy and compassion: if assessing emotions is troublesome for you, continue to build your practice with the 360 Librarian ideal of Empathetic Reflection (chapter 4). With practice, you'll be able to empathize with other people and yourself, making it easier to set aside your own emotional entanglements and approach communication with kindness toward yourself and others.

Case study, continued: At the reference desk, the student stood before Eugene, waiting to hear if he would assist her. He really wanted to go home and briefly had the uncharitable thought that if the student hadn't procrastinated, then maybe she wouldn't be in this situation—and should this be the opportunity for a hard life lesson for this student? He looked at the student's hands, which were still trembling. She spoke in a staccato frenzy, like she wanted to run away from this thing that scared her. After assessing the student's emotional state, Eugene knew they had to sit down for a consultation. This student was overwhelmed by her upcoming presentation, frustrated by her inability to find source material and possibly nervous about asking for help. In fact, she never used the word *help* or even posed a question when she approached the reference desk but rather stated her project and information need. Upon later reflection, Eugene realized she may not have ever asked for help at the library before.

Reacting to emotions

Managing and regulating emotions begins the moment we awake in the morning and continues throughout the day. More than the simple practice of stoicism or equanimity, this step contains the deep awareness that positive and negative emotions are bubbling under the surface of all our interactions. Emotional Awareness allows us to act, and react, with the full understanding that while we are not in charge of someone else's initial emotional reaction to an event or interaction, we are in charge of our own reactions to our own and other people's emotions. We can use our emotional reactions to positively influence events and, to a certain extent, nudge other people toward more positive emotions.

As mentioned previously, emotions can easily be influenced by those around us. For example, walking into a classroom, instructors can typically get a feel for the mood of those in the room. On any given day, a librarian may do as many as three instruction sessions for the same course with the same professor, yet each class will have a distinctly unique mood and personality. You might have experienced a time when you have been in engaged in a light-hearted conversation with coworkers when a more serious coworker stops by and your emotions and the emotions of your conversation partners are suddenly hijacked and the mood turns somber.

Positively influencing events and emotions as a general practice might seem to insinuate that the reacting aspect of Emotional Awareness is submissive in nature: soothing, capitulating, agreeing, cheerleading. We want to echo Daniel Goleman here and be very clear that being emotionally intelligent and practicing Emotional Awareness does not equate to being weak or submissive.[19] Emotional Awareness is a way of consciously affecting the outcome of events while retaining your own equanimity. This difficult practice involves a range of emotions and actions which others may label as "tough," "soft," "good," "bad," or "emotional," and so on, but this labeling is their practice, not yours.

The motivation for emotional regulation and action varies depending on our environment and social partners. Emotion regulation can be internally motivated by a desire "to increase or maintain pleasure and to decrease negative emotions."[20] In the library and for other service professions, emotional regulation can be externally motivated by what the service industry refers to as "customer service interaction display rules," illustrated by chestnuts like "service with a smile" and "the customer is king." The expectation to expend emotional labor during customer service is part of a manager's expectation for employees to monitor and regulate their emotions during any professional interaction.[21] In a 360 Librarian practice, emotional regulation is motivated by a desire to integrate a mindful presence with high-level calm communication while exceeding student and colleague expectations.

Do the practice: Observe the mood and energy in as many group settings as you can: committee meetings, department meetings, instruction sessions, hallway chats, lunchroom talk, and even email chains. How does the mood and energy in one group setting differ from another? What or whom do you contribute this difference to? Does one person in the group tend to be the emotional leader? Is it hierarchical? Is it topical? Is it because of longstanding rivalries? How can the mood be influenced or changed?

Do the practice: Decide on an interaction you would like to influence and take the role of emotional leader. Using conversational skills outlined in chapter 3, Engaged Communication, align yourself with your conversational partner or with the larger group. Remember that good conversations tend to align physiological rhythms, and invest yourself in finding out more about the other person's emotional state. Pay attention to subtle nonverbal clues such as a flushed face, trembling hands, poor eye contact. Are they scared, confused, or frightened? Angry? Frustrated? Keeping in mind that emotions are contagious, do not take negative emotions into your own mindstate, but try to calmly investigate the cause. Practice empathetic listening and engage in conversation that focuses on positivity and reduces the toxicity of the situation, therefore elevating the mood to attune with your desired state.

Case study, continued: As a service provider, Eugene knew he could overlook his small irritations about the timing of this question. Instead, he found he could empathize with this student—he definitely knew what it was like to procrastinate! Eugene knew there could be any number of reasons for her procrastination, from a misunderstanding about the assignment, to long hours put in at work to pay for college, or other personal or academic issues. Turning to the student, Eugene took a deep breath and saw her do the same. He smiled, and her hands stopped visibly shaking. He offered her a seat and told the student he would be happy to help get her started. Her relief was palpable as she explained her project to him in greater detail. Eugene assured the student the library had many articles on her topic and within moments she was confidently poring over the database results list.

Integrating Emotional Awareness

Emotionally aware librarians lead by staying in tune with their own feelings and histories instead of adopting a leadership framework for the moment. Adopting the leadership style of another person, even if it's trending leadership and management styles of the most celebrated leaders, often leads to a lack of authenticity and creates a dissonance that results in a disconnect and a lack of trust among colleagues. In contrast, those who resonate with their colleagues lead from authentic values they gained from the successes and failures experienced throughout life. In *Harvard Business Review*, Bill George describes such authentic leaders as people who "lead with their hearts as well as their heads. They establish long-term, meaningful relationships and… they know who they are."[22] Each of these characteristics requires a facility with elements of Goleman's Emotional Intelligence framework.

To *lead with the heart* is a noticing practice that requires a rich store of empathy to consider the feelings and needs of others, a willingness to develop and bolster others in the workplace, and the ability to take an active interest in others' well-being. Recognizing emotions, perspective taking, and listening are just some of the "heart" qualities that create resonance with colleagues. Those who lead with the heart are attuned to not only their own emotional signals but also those of their colleagues,[23] creating an atmosphere of understanding and inclusion. With the knowledge gleaned from genuinely taking an interest in their colleagues, adept leaders become intimately aware of colleagues' strengths, weaknesses, and ambitions.[24] This awareness creates an opportunity for authentic leadership when mentoring and coaching their colleagues, followed by an opportunity to celebrate the hard-earned achievements of their colleagues.

To *establish long-term meaningful relationships* is a reacting practice that requires the social competence to skillfully manage conflict, listen and respond with meaningful intent, and to purposefully build strong bonds with colleagues. Influential leaders have engaging personalities and are able to find support and create buy-in from key people. As they inspire others, a culture of collegiality is created. Mindfully engaging with colleagues translates into an ability to act as a catalyst for change when recognizing where similarities and differences amongst co-workers arise. Using this inside knowledge, leaders are able to observe and acknowledge all sides of an argument and move energy and expertise toward a solution that incorporates each employee's strengths.

To *know who they are* is an assessing practice of personal competence in order to manage oneself and have the self-awareness to recognize one's own emotions and consider how they may impact others. This practice requires the ability to regulate emotions and take personal responsibility for one's own actions while leading with principle and sincerity. Self-confidence and self-control are at the center of competence. Self-confidence allows leaders to reflect on their past accomplishments, successful or otherwise, and then openly and transparently share and use these experiences as a basis to build the future. Leaders who know who they are openly admit mistakes, confront unethical behavior, and are graceful under pressure.[25]

ENDNOTES

1. Daniel Goleman, *Working with Emotional Intelligence* (New York: Bantam Books, 2000).
2. Goleman, *Working with Emotional Intelligence*.
3. Trevor Foulk, Andrew Woolum, and Amir Erez, "Catching Rudeness is Like Catching a Cold: The Contagion Effects of Low-Intensity Negative Behaviors," *Journal of Applied Psychology* 101, no. 1 (2016).
4. Peter Salovey and John D. Mayer, "Emotional Intelligence," *Imagination, Cognition and Personality* 9, no. 3 (March 1990): 185.
5. Maya Tamir, "The Maturing Field of Emotion Regulation," *Emotion Review* 3, no. 1 (January 2011): 3, http://journals.sagepub.com/doi/abs/10.1177/1754073910388685?-journalCode=.
6. Goleman, *Working with Emotional Intelligence*, 167.
7. Daniel Goleman, Richard Boyatzis, and Annie McKee, "Primal Leadership: The Hidden Driver of Great Performance," *Harvard Business Review* 79, no. 11 (December 2001).
8. Goleman, Boyatzis, and McKee, "Primal Leadership."
9. Ibid.
10. Goleman, *Working with Emotional Intelligence*, 243.
11. Ibid.
12. Travis Bradberry and Jean Greaves, *Emotional Intelligence 2.0: The World's Most Popular Emotional Intelligence Test* (San Diego, CA: TalentSmart, 2009).
13. Bradberry and Jean Greaves, *Emotional Intelligence 2.0*.
14. Anna Maravelas, *How to Reduce Workplace Conflict and Stress: How Leaders and Their Employees Can Protect Their Sanity and Productivity from Tension and Turf Wars* (Franklin Lakes, NJ: Career Press, 2005).
15. Goleman, *Working with Emotional Intelligence*, 61.
16. Lisa Feldman Barrett, *How Emotions Are Made: The Secret Life of the Brain* (Boston: Houghton Mifflin Harcourt, 2017), 195.
17. Joan Giesecke, "Emotional Intelligence," in *Academic Librarians as Emotionally Intelligent Leaders*, eds. Peter Hernon, Joan Giesecke, and Camila A. Alire (Westport, CT: Libraries Unlimited, 2007), 6.
18. Giesecke, "Emotional Intelligence."

19. Daniel Goleman, Richard Boyatzis, and Annie McKee, *Primal Leadership: Realizing the Power of Emotional Intelligence* (Boston: Harvard Business School Press, 2002).
20. Laura von Gilsa et al., "There is More than Obeying Display Rules: Service Employees' Motives for Emotion Regulation in Customer Interactions," *European Journal of Work and Organizational Psychology* 23, no. 6 (November 2014): 885, https://doi.org/10.1080/1359432X.2013.839548.
21. Gilsa et al., "There Is More."
22. Bill George et al., "Discovering Your Authentic Leadership," *Harvard Business Review* 85, no. 2 (February 2007): 130.
23. Goleman, Boyatzis, and McKee, *Primal Leadership: Realizing.*
24. Ibid.
25. Ibid.

CHAPTER 3

Engaged Communication

The third 360 Librarian ideal, Engaged Communication, consists of awareness of nonverbal communication, the practice of deep listening, and deliberate two-way communication. We have previously described Engaged Communication as a "multifaceted act" that we present here as at once contemplative and active, easeful and determined. Engaged Communication is the midway point between the internally-focused Mindful Practice and Emotional Awareness and the more externally-focused 360 ideals of Empathetic Reflection and Action and Reassurance. Librarians who become proficient at Engaged Communication in the workplace can quickly build rapport with colleagues and patrons, establishing relationships that reduce uncertainty and enable confident information sharing.

Engaged Communication is a purposeful connection, the elements of which bring ease and authenticity to the challenging act of remaining fully engaged with an interaction partner. The process of interpreting gestures, body language, and style and tone of speech as a part of communication allows 360 Librarians to place their interactions into a richer context in order to react more appropriately to any given situation. An engaged workplace culture establishes space for authentic connection that allows members of the team to reflect on the emotional and physical state of others and then have the self-confidence to candidly assess feedback being given or received at that moment. With a continual practice of Engaged Communication, 360 Librarians can use their deepening understanding of verbal and nonverbal cues to influence and motivate others in their organization and their community to remain positive and proactive when solving problems or undertaking new projects.

Practicing Engaged Communication

Through the practice of Engaged Communication, you are learning new ways to connect with others in the physical world through your senses. Although they are all parts of the communication process, the three elements of this ideal tend to be embodied and expressed so differently that they may seem like disparate acts. If that is the case for you, it may be most helpful to understand and practice each element separately at first. The acts of watching, listening, and speaking carefully will naturally come together over time, leading to a clear practice of interconnected engagement.

In contrast to the quiet and inward-facing Mindful Practice and Emotional Awareness ideals, Engaged Communication may feel direct and sometimes even contentious as you become adept at nonverbal communication, practice deep listening, and take part in deliberate two-way communications. As you begin noticing others more fully and try to place them first in the conversation, there may be a natural tendency for your own mind to chatter and make itself known. Acknowledge and become aware of your own nonverbal cues of when you are not listening or when you're overbearing in conversations so you can gently unwind and release these unhelpful habits from your communication style.

Nonverbal communication

Observation of nonverbal signals are crucial to interpreting and facilitating communication and are the key to a mindful 360 Librarian process. The value of nonverbal signals is most apparent when those signals are absent. Without additional nonverbal context and subsequent additional meaning, the 360-degree communication process slows or stops completely. Nonverbal signals were one of the first forms of human communication and tend to be what we notice first when communicating with others. In fact, when verbal and nonverbal messages are at odds, our tendency is to rely on nonverbal messages more heavily than verbal messages to decipher the true intentions and meaning of interactions. Once nonverbal and verbal messages begin to correspond, we rely more heavily on the information shared via the verbal channel.[1] For instance, if a smiling patron requests to speak to an administrator, you may be confused when they begin to lodge a complaint about the fines on their account. To most of us, smiling connotes a positive message which is at odds with a complaint. Similarly, when a frowning patron approaches to compliment you on the library's most recent program you may be taken aback for a moment as the nonverbal cues were clearly expressing discontent toward you.

Spoken words tend to take priority when communicating "factual, abstract, and persuasive" messages and the nonverbal channel takes primacy for "messages related to impressions, relationships, and affective states."[2] Whether or not we are cognizant of it, the subtle physiological and emotional cues that emanate during social interactions play a key role in first impressions and relationship management.[3] The frowning patron in your library, then, is most likely actually stating their support for that program, even as they called up an impression of dislike for the library.

> *Do the practice:* Reflect on a time when you were communicating with a person whose facial expressions or body language—their nonverbal message—did not match their verbal message. Why do you think their messages were not synced? Which message did you believe? Was it hard to follow the conversation? How did you react? Did you ask for clarification? Did the incongruent messages affect your response?

Behaviors expressing mood or emotion such as facial expressions (smiles or frowns), body language (crossing the arms or legs), gaze (looking around or directly at the speaker), posture (slouching or standing tall), vocal intonation (shrill or soothing), and gestures (pointing or waving the hands) are nonverbal communication cues that help decipher and add perspective to a social interaction. Nonverbal cues play a role in fulfilling communicative goals such as building new relationships, creating a positive self-image, and decoding sincerity or deceit.[4] Back in the library, you can probably tell that a smiling patron is intent on building rapport with you and projecting a calm, confident, sincere demeanor as they make their case for getting their fines forgiven.

> *Do the practice:* With a partner or using a mirror, attempt a mismatched verbal message and facial expression. For instance, talk about a raise without smiling, or tell a story about your pet misbehaving with a smile. Have your partner interpret what they thought of as the "real" message. Next, retell the story and match the expression to the verbal message. Share your news about a raise with a smile and maybe a high-five. Your pet misbehaving brings pursed lips and a shake of the head. How does that change the interpreta-

tion of the event from the sender's (you) and receiver's (your partner) point of view?

Mindful engagement in an emotionally aware conversation requires the ability to encode and decode nonverbal messages as they occur. Paul Ekman, a pioneer in the study of emotions and their relation to facial expressions, writes that careful attention to one's conversation partner reduces the risk of misinterpretation of the intended message. Furthermore, being aware of your own emotional reactions during a conversation creates the mental space needed to view exchanges from our communication partner's perspective.[5] For you, frowns come in with complaints all day. For your patron who enjoys the teen programs, their facial expression may be completely unrelated to your interaction. Anything from a momentary lapse of thought to a naturally negative expression could be the reason for their frown. It's up to you, then, to separate the frown from the compliment and react appropriately, with pleasure, to the exchange.

One powerful instrument of emotional intelligence is the ability to read people by noticing and interpreting their facial expression and nonverbal signals.[6] Subtle cues help reduce misinterpretations during social interactions. We decode back-channel communication like head tilts, a wrinkled nose, a furrowed brow, among other cues, to gain a complete picture of what is being communicated during each interaction. Admittedly, some people are difficult to read. They may not react with facial expressions as someone else is speaking or they may listen intently without, for instance, nodding or shaking their head to signify approval or disagreement. For these people, it may be more helpful to shift the decoding to a verbal medium by simply asking, "What is your opinion on this matter?" or "What do you think about this news?" If that seems too forward, try to be even more perceptive of their nonverbal cues.

Strengthen your emotional intelligence, particularly your social competence in empathy, by recognizing back-channel communication during conversations. Acknowledging back-channel communication and nonverbal signals as another element of the conversation is an opportunity to gain insight and show concern for your communication partner's well-being. Nonverbal signals such as facial expression, body language, posture, gestures, breathing rate, and eye contact offer clues into the emotional state of the speaker and offer a chance for you to align yourself, nonverbally or verbally, with them. Remember, communication partners can align emotionally during conversation, even if they are strangers. The same is undoubtedly true for nonverbal communication as well. Those who are in alliance will typically engage in conversation within close proximity of each other, may mimic the posture and body language of their colleague, and may even engage in knowing glances. Head nodding, smiling, eye contact, and raised eyebrows are signals of cooperation. Disagreement or animosity can be displayed with poor eye contact, a furrowed brow, and closed body language such as folded arms. Confusion or distrust may be signaled with squinting eyes, the head tipped to one side or shaking, and the hand covering the mouth.[7]

Do the practice: To understand someone else's nonverbal cues, spend time watching other people's conversations from across the room or turn on the television at home without the sound. Pay attention to their nonverbal behavior and back channel communication. How long does it take for facial expressions to be shared in groups? What makes people lean in or away from the speaker? How do listeners receive nonverbal messages like crossed arms or legs?

Do the practice: To align your own nonverbal cues with your spoken message, use a mirror to watch yourself speak. See what happens to your eyes, nose, and mouth when you say certain things normally and then when you mismatch your verbal and nonverbal messages on purpose. Mix and match the verbal messages and the back-channel communications below to see how your actual message may get misconstrued by a mere slip of the face.

Verbal messages
- "I'm so happy to meet you."
- "I disagree with your assessment of the situation."
- "What you say makes me uncomfortable, and I would like you to stop."
- "You are a valued part of this organization."
- "I'm disappointed by our lack of participation in this effort."
- "I look forward to working with you on this project."

Back-channel communication
- Smiling *or* frowning
- Arms folded in front *or* on hips
- Looking down *or* maintaining eye contact
- Hands open in front *or* finger pointing
- Sharp intake of breath *or* calm exhalation

Case study: Kamilla was a new librarian who was expected to attend department meetings every week. Never before having attended department meetings as a librarian, she was unsure of her role in the meetings and often stayed silent throughout the meeting. Occasionally, she was confused by acronyms and lost when discussion turned to institutional history. Instead of asking in the meeting, she took notes on these things to look up or ask about later and, like some of the other librarians, spoke only when the discussion turned to her area of expertise in the library. Kamilla noticed that there were a few librarians who dominated the meetings, interrupting or talking over others in order to get their points across and projects approved. Kamilla thought the librarians in her department didn't want to work together because only a few of them made eye contact with one another, and some of them even sighed or rolled their eyes when others were speaking. She knew there must be a better way to communicate during department meetings and promote equity and camaraderie in the meetings.

Kamilla was often nervous during these meetings. She thought of herself as a confident person, though, and was confused by her negative feelings surrounding this one event during the week. Thinking about her colleagues, she wondered if they were aware of how their communication styles were affecting other people in the room. Kamilla recognized that she was having difficulty interpreting one of her colleague's nonverbal cues, as they tended to speak quietly, without gesturing. Another colleague had a very dry sense of humor and often cracked jokes that didn't seem funny to her. The meetings were close to lunchtime, so Kamilla knew that many of her colleagues came to the meeting hungry. Kamilla wanted to change her actions in the meetings and speak up for herself and the other people in the room who were being silenced. She wanted to speak carefully and thoughtfully and establish some ground rules for respectful communication during the meeting.

Deep listening

The practice of Engaged Communication continues with deep listening. Listening deeply requires what Daniel Barbezat and Mirabai Bush call a "contemplative mind: open, fresh, alert, attentive, calm, and receptive."[8] Practicing Engaged Communication has thus far enabled you to "listen" to nonverbal communication; the observation of nonverbal cues combined with deep listening creates the space needed to decipher emotions and intention. This enables you to *understand*.

Deep listening is a dynamic process of de-emphasizing your ego while listening in order to delve into the feelings, emotions, and intentions behind someone else's words. The process of deep listening creates an opportunity to practice empathy and demonstrate compassion for others. When we take on the role of listener, it is common for us to try to "judge, fix, blame, control, help, criticize, or rescue" our communication partner with our thoughts or speech.[9] Mindful, engaged, and emotionally aware listening eliminates those negative thoughts. It decentralizes a self-centered "I can help" or "I can fix this" attitude in favor of a patient, other-centered interaction. It brings a service orientation to all communication, rather than just the moments of interaction behind a public desk.

The most important step to deep listening is to pay full attention to what the other person is saying. Hear their words without judging them. Cease thinking about your own narrative in relation to theirs. This practice may be challenging at first but will most likely feel more natural as your attention develops. Deep listening meshes well with a deeper understanding of the first 360 Librarian ideal, Mindful Practice. As your mind is able to focus without distractions, your listening skills will sharpen.

> *Do the practice (with someone else):* With a trusted partner, become more aware of your own meandering thoughts while someone else is speaking. Have your partner tell a story or read from a book. Open your mind to their words and receive them without relating them to yourself. Every time you think of ways to judge, fix, blame, control, help, criticize, or rescue your partner, raise your hand. Change roles so everyone is the speaker and listener at least once.

> *Do the practice (by yourself):* The difficult practice of deep listening may be especially hard for those of us with anxiety or attention-related diagnoses. Be kind to yourself while completing this exercise and consider beginning the practice by yourself instead. If you have the opportunity, attend a public lecture. Or, in the privacy of your home, download a podcast. Follow the content of the lecture or podcast. Try to notice when you think of ways to judge, fix, blame, control, help, criticize, or rescue the speaker. Critiquing the content is acceptable, especially if you do it with a spirit of generous curiosity. When your mind wanders or you begin to do the closed thinking listed above, take a breath and return your mind to the speaker. Do this as much as you need to during the entire lecture or podcast.

In addition to openly and nonjudgmentally listening to the words someone is saying, listen for paralanguage that, along with nonverbal and verbal communication, completes the picture of communication. Paralanguage, much like back-channel communication, is the individual speech characteristics that each person uses while they speak: ums, ahs, and pauses along with pitch, speed, and style.[10] This can often indicate whether or not the mental state of the speaker matches the words they say.

Deep listening sometimes requires you, the listener, to engage in paralanguage of your own to continue the interaction in a positive and authentic manner. Pay careful attention to the signals you are sharing with your communication partner to ensure you are accepting their message. This doesn't mean you have to agree with the information being shared but indicates you are accepting that verbal communication is occurring and you are listening in order to facilitate open, effective, authentic communication. To indicate acceptance, don't interrupt the speaker. Instead, use back-channel cues, like a nod or raising your eyebrows, to encourage them to continue speaking. Interruptions may occur for reasons as benign as a time crunch or as malevolent as bullying or a need to assert superiority. Regardless of the intent, interruptions derail civil, engaged, two-way communication. If you're prone to interrupting, acknowledge that this is an area of development for yourself and practice patience. Suspend your critical thoughts, the need to fix the situation, or the need to control the outcome while conversing with colleagues. Rather, practice verbal responses ("Yes," "Mmhmm," "Go on,") that affirms understanding and encourages the speaker to elaborate on their idea.[11]

In the 360 ideal of Engaged Communication, we separate deep listening from active listening. Active listening is a communication method commonly taught in psychology or counseling that includes paraphrasing what your communication partner says in a proactive and respectful manner. A communication partner who is actively listening to a colleague venting about a new university policy may say such things as, "It seems like you're frustrated by this new policy, is that right? I really hear you saying that you think your concerns weren't adequately taken into consideration when the administration made the new policy. Can you tell me more about that?"

In Engaged Communication, interactions like these are the purview of two-way communication and may take a similar tone. Deep listening, as a practice completely separate from responding in any way, enables you to engage with your communication partner in a completely open, nonjudgmental manner, without adhering to the "rules" of active listening. A communication partner listening deeply to the colleague above would partake in a process receiving and perceiving the conversation as a series of moments in which to be curious about the feelings and perceptions of another person. Someone who is practicing deep listening would, in addition to listening to the words their colleague is speaking, also notice their folded arms, furrowed brow, and sarcastic or angry tone of voice. They would note that their colleague is speaking faster than usual, or louder than usual, and punctuates their words with large sighs.

Do the practice: Try to practice an active deep listening as long as you can in one day. In everyday conversation, turn your mind to the stories of others instead of your own. Listen with curiosity. Notice what is left unspoken yet is essential to the story. What emotions are being evoked? How is your communication partner's experience different than your own? Is there an unspoken moment of connection, a feeling that you're on "the same page," that has been noticed by you and your communication partner? When someone shares an anecdote, ask them at least one question about their story. If you are at a loss for questions, just say, "Tell me more." Most importantly, try not to share your own anecdotes during the day, especially in a mindless loop of tangentially related stories. For one day, listen more and speak less.

Case study, continued: Once she decided to change the way she communicated in department meetings, Kamilla began to listen deeply. She understood that each colleague had a unique perspective on the politics and culture within the library, and a few had a long history of service at the institution. There were as many perspectives as there were colleagues—each attending and participating in the meetings through their individual lens. When she listened to the topics under discussion and the way in which they were discussed at each meeting, her perception about the negativity in each meeting shifted. She understood that all her colleagues cared deeply about the students who visited the library. When they spoke about students, they smiled, made eye contact, and used positive language. Kamilla was able to relate to her colleagues in these moments. Knowing that some of her colleagues interrupted people and others sighed sometimes, Kamilla also listened to other methods of communication. Looking around the table one day, she noticed that all of her colleagues had their arms at their sides or their hands folded in front of them in a nonthreatening manner. None of them crossed their arms or clenched their hands together tightly. Even when they were engaging in what Kamilla perceived as argumentative communication, their body language didn't reflect animosity or judgment.

Deliberate two-way communication

As with the other elements of Engaged Communication, deliberate two-way communication is a learned skill that diverts the ego away from waiting to be heard and instead concentrates all our energy on the other person's ideas. This enables us to gain understanding from multiple perspectives in addition to viewing the conversation through our lens. Paying attention to details, emotions, and nonverbal signals increase clarity and help to more fully understand the situation at hand. This leads to informed decision-making, superior customer service, and improved collegial relationships.

Deliberate two-way communication combines nonverbal communication and deep listening with your verbal reactions to indicate to your communication partner that you are present and vested in the conversation. In "Reference 360," we noted that many patrons appeared keenly aware when one-way communication occurs during conversations with an inattentive librarian. Inattentiveness can be caused by external and internal factors like discomfort with physical surroundings, a line of students waiting for help, errant thoughts about work completed or yet to come, or emotional leftovers from workplace or personal issues. Deliberate two-way communication involves mutual attunement and focused engagement of our senses in order to limit distractions and improve understanding. Challenging as it may be, the ability to be fully present, nonjudgmentally, begins to turn one-way interactions that are initiated and closed entirely by the patron into successful examples of two-way communication.[12]

> *Do the practice:* To identify and minimize physical distractions, do a body scan. Starting at the top of your head, send your awareness to your muscle groups. If any are tense, breathe into them, and ask those muscles to relax. Are you carrying tension in your neck or back? This is a common problem for people who sit at desks much of the day. During a break, try a few sitting desk stretches.

> *Do the practice:* To minimize distractions caused by thoughts or emotions that can be managed or set aside during your workday, try to identify those thoughts or emotions before they spiral out of control. When you feel overwhelmed, discouraged, sad, or angry, stop and take a deep breath. Remind yourself that it's okay to feel however you're feeling. If you aren't in a good place or time to fully investigate or experience those feelings, note where and when you will be able to explore your thoughts and emotions. If needed, write down your thoughts in a safe place, such as a personal email to yourself or in your 360 Journal or a notetaking app on your phone. Finally, look for a positive side to the situation to take you back to your professional sphere.

If you remain distracted by sensations or external events that are readily apparent to your communication partner, it can be helpful to verbalize the distraction, even if this brings your communication partner's attention to the event as well. If it is combined with a short apology and reassurance that you are now attending to their message, verbalizing obvious external distractions can build rapport between you and your patron. For instance, at a service desk with uncomfortable physical surroundings, you might say, "Oh, I just noticed a buzzing light. Forgive me for being thrown off for a moment. What was your question?" Even internal distractions can be verbalized, but take care to ensure the conversation does not involve your physical or mental health. For instance, as a consultation begins, you might say, "I'm sorry, I just read an email about a completely different topic, so my head needs a brief moment to catch up. Can you tell me more about your research?" With a co-worker, if you have serious internal distractions that aren't readily apparent you may ask to make an appointment to speak with them at a different time or place. Again, it is not necessary to specify the nature of your distraction, "I'm sorry, Jill. A few things have conspired against me this morning, so I can't concentrate as much as I'd like to on our conversation right now. Are you on a deadline, or can we chat about the budget later this afternoon?"

Deliberate two-way communication requires crafting coherent positive verbal and nonverbal messages by cueing into social and emotional signals during conversations and carefully choosing words and the tone in which a message is delivered. It is an active process containing affirming language that encourages meaningful dialogue. Dismissive language, interruptions, and a negative or sarcastic tone of voice discourage kind and intellectual discourse and places an immediate barrier between you and your communication partner.

> *Do the practice*: Choose your words carefully. Take special notice of the words and phrases you use most often at work. Make a list. Highlight the words and phrases that have positive connotations and cross out the ones that have negative connotations. Come up with positive versions of your most-used negative phrases. Even the word "no" can be uttered with a warm tone and a smile, turning a possible negative interaction into a neutral one.

Case study, continued: At the next meeting, Kamilla decided to speak up during a contentious discussion. She realized early on in the meeting that she was gritting her teeth and feeling overwhelmed by the interruptions that were happening during this discussion. Before speaking, she took a deep breath and unclenched her jaw. She sat up in her chair and stretched her back slightly to minimize the physical discomfort she brought into the meeting. Silently, she acknowledged that the discussion was a little overwhelming but that she would process her feelings about the situation after work in her journal. During a pause in the discussion, Kamilla spoke. "I can't help but notice that we all feel passionate about this topic. Thankfully, we're all on the same page about how much we care for our students' experience here at the library. Instead of talking over each other and voting for one single solution, I would like to list all our ideas on one sheet and look for commonalities. I believe we can come up with a great solution together." Kamilla took the opportunity during the same meeting to establish a framework for problem-solving, which included brainstorming solutions for policy questions together as a team.

Integrating Engaged Communication

Engaged Communication can be challenging in a workplace that appears to shun connection either on purpose through political maneuvering or bullying or accidentally through overworked or introverted coworkers. If you must hide in your office for self-preservation or are unable to connect with your colleagues for anything other than a quick greeting in the morning, then your first forays into Engaged Communication may have to take place outside your library or concentrate solely on your interactions with your patrons.

Creating connection when people around you seem to be perpetually disconnected does take a series of committed and decisive steps toward honest and open communication. Luckily, the first few steps in Engaged Communication are nonverbal and internal and, once mastered, can fortify your resolve to solve problems using deliberate two-way communication. We hope that a continual practice of the many facets of engaged communication, even in a disconnected workplace, can create an atmosphere of understanding and collegiality where communication partners can work toward mutual goals. Even with intractable or irascible colleagues, practicing equanimity and responding authentically in all communication ensures that problems are solved roughly equitably and with more ease than unhappiness.

We know that Engaged Communication is not easy in a fast-paced, distracted world. Slowing down and mindfully responding to the verbal and nonverbal cues of your communication partner builds empathy and significantly improves the quality of your interactions. This deliberate act empowers your communication partner to fully express their needs and reduces the frustration that can occur when communication is interrupted. Whether it is finding the courage to artfully engage in a contentious interaction or ensuring your communication partner truly feels heard, a calm and mindful presence during every interaction leads to rewarding and fulfilling conversations.

ENDNOTES

1. Judee K. Burgoon, Laura K. Guerrero, and Valerie Manusov, "Nonverbal Signals," in *The Sage Handbook of Interpersonal Communication*, 4th ed., eds. Mark L. Knapp and John A. Daly (Thousand Oaks: SAGE, 2011).
2. Burgoon, Guerrero, and Manusov, "Nonverbal Signals," 242.
3. Ibid.
4. Ibid.
5. Paul Ekman, *Emotions Revealed: Recognizing Faces and Feelings to Improve Communication and Emotional Life* (New York: St. Martin's Griffin, 2003).
6. David Ricky Matsumoto, Mark G. Frank, and Hyi Sung Hwang, "Reading People: Introduction to the World of Nonverbal Behavior," in *Nonverbal Communication: Science and Applications*, eds. David Ricky Matsumoto, Mark G. Frank, and Hyi Sung Hwang (Los Angeles: SAGE, 2013).
7. Adrian Furnham and Evgeniya Petrova, *Body Language in Business: Decoding the Signals* (Basingstoke, Hampshire, UK: Palgrave Macmillan, 2010).
8. Daniel Barbezat and Mirabai Bush, *Contemplative Practices in Higher Education: Powerful Methods to Transform Teaching and Learning* (San Francisco: Jossey-Bass, 2014), 138.
9. Randy Fujishin, *Creating Effective Groups: The Art of Small Group Communication*, 2nd ed. (Lanham, MD: Rowman & Littlefield, 2007), 57.
10. Patricia Dewdney and Gillian Michell, "Oranges and Peaches: Understanding Communication Accidents in the Reference Interview," *RQ* 35, no. 4 (July 1996).
11. Fujishin, *Creating Effective Groups*.
12. Carol A. Daul-Elhindi and Tammi M. Owens, "Reference 360: A Holistic Approach to Reference Instruction," in *Teaching Reference Today: New Directions, Novel Approaches*, ed. Lisa A. Ellis (Lanham: Rowman & Littlefield, 2016).

CHAPTER 4

Empathetic Reflection and Action

The fourth 360 Librarian ideal is Empathetic Reflection and Action. We have previously defined this as the ability to reflect on the interpersonal interaction *as it happens*, staying in tune with one's intuition regarding the other person's information need and current state of mind and responding in a considerate and appropriate manner in light of these reflections. Our first conception of this ideal was for a single encounter at a service desk during a reference interaction; however, Empathetic Reflection and Action can and will occur throughout a 360 Librarian's workday as they attend meetings, speak with colleagues, interact with patrons, and more. It isn't necessary to use empathetic reflection during every interaction every day, but authentic intentional communication has the opportunity to occur in greater measure when practicing this ideal.

The components of Empathetic Reflection and Action are, on their face, easily laid bare: empathy, reflection, and action. There is a freshness about the simplicity in interpersonal communication led by these components marching forward from one to the other, in that order. Staying mindfully in the moment, use your natural empathy to listen actively to both the verbal and physical cues your conversation partner is sending, reflect on the moment at hand, and take some sort of action at that moment using both implicit and tacit knowledge of your field or the knowledge you hold of the situation before you. Practicing the ideal in this manner is an intellectual endeavor that can be internalized with a sensitive workflow. For instance, you can easily infer that a patron who arrives at the service desk with their books and library card in hand is in a hurry to catch the bus if they are looking out the door toward the bus stop and rummaging in their bag for change. Your empathetic reflection and action may simply be to quickly and efficiently check out their books and ensure they catch their bus on time.

Continual practice of structured interactions, such as the service desk scenario described above, is one avenue into an intuitive practice of Empathetic Reflection and Action. Another avenue into Empathetic Reflection and Action is to understand and practice the individual components of the ideal, each of which has a relationship to one of the first three ideals of the 360 Framework. Empathy is one aspect of Emotional Awareness, reflection is a Mindful Practice, and action takes careful and decisive Engaged Communication. The practice of each component separately, then together, then finally as related to the whole of the 360 Framework, enables a deep practice of Empathetic Reflection and Action as a continuous state. In this state, you can create macro or micro changes in yourself, your team, your organization, or your community at large.

Three Parts of One Ideal
Empathy

Empathy is the ability to identify, understand, and relate to the emotional state of another person.[1] It is both a neurological process and an intuitive skill that can be developed further with training. With an inward turn, empathy can also incorporate the idea of self-compassion. By learning to recognize and harness empathy for this ideal, 360 Librarians will be more prepared to integrate the Emotional Awareness ideal into their everyday practice of the 360 Framework.

Philosophers and psychologists have been debating and refining the definitions of empathy since the eighteenth-century moral philosophy of David Hume and Adam Smith. Today, researchers typically acknowledge two main types of empathy: affective and cognitive.[2] Affective empathy refers to the physical sensations that we experience and adopt in response to the emotions of people around us. It is the idea, first proposed by Hume and called sympathy, later labeled "emotional contagion" by Hatfield et al., that a person can mirror and then "catch" another person's emotional state.[3] Cognitive empathy is a more creative mental exercise. Described by Smith as "changing places in fancy" or "fellow feeling," it is the ability to recognize and imagine what someone may be thinking or feeling in a situation and putting oneself in that place.[4] For this 360 Librarian ideal, we hew closely to the cognitive model of empathy as we champion the practice of intuiting another person's thoughts or feelings without being disproportionately affected by them.

The practice of Empathetic Reflection and Action, in whole or in part, may be difficult for 360 Librarians with a self-defeating inner dialogue. Shame, guilt, fear, or lack of confidence may make it difficult to reflect with kindness on situations in the workplace. For those who struggle with negative self-talk, empathetic feeling may be used on the self as readily as it is on others. Kristin D. Neff describes self-empathy as the mindful practice of self-compassion or kindness toward oneself. Neff writes that in order to be self-compassionate, people must, among other practices, distance themselves from their own suffering and connect to the suffering of others by acknowledging the interdependence of all humanity.[5]

360 Librarians practicing deep empathy should keep self-compassion and self-care at the forefront of their service and resist the urge to capitulate to controlling or self-serving people. Patrons, colleagues, and students may mistake empathetic practice for weakness and seek to take advantage of simple kindnesses. Sympathy, which is a "feeling of care or concern for others," especially in commiseration with events or situations that may be perceived as negative or unhelpful, is often mistaken for empathy.[6] Sympathy engenders feeling but typically does not elicit *shared* feeling and is thus not the aim of this ideal. Regardless, neither empathy nor sympathy require accepting rude complaints, making considerable or constant exceptions to policies and procedures, or letting others take precedence to the detriment of your career or equanimity. Empathy is a kind expansion of one's self, not a diminishing into another person's difficulties.

Engaging in the empathetic behavior of listening, observing, and accurately perceiving emotion in yourself and in others is also a foundational skill required for emotional awareness. Emotional Awareness and Empathetic Reflection and Action both require the personal competence to reflect on and manage one's own emotional state as well as the social competence to intuitively understand another's thoughts and emotions, regardless of whether you think and feel the same. For many people, empathy comes naturally but in varying degrees. A two-step exercise can help strengthen the "empathy reflex." First, reflect on the emotional state of your coworker. Take time to consider events that may have led up to the emotional response. For example, did a coworker's frustration during a contentious conversation earlier in the day with a supervisor cause unwarranted negativity seeping into an interaction during a department meeting? Second, reflect on the basis of the emotional reaction. Does your coworker feel undervalued or unheard within the department or by the supervisor?[7]

Recognizing and understanding the emotions of others is only the beginning of the empathy component of Empathetic Reflection and Action. Once your empathy reflex is strong and understanding other people comes more naturally, engage with others to communicate your empathetic feelings to them. Instead of leaving someone alone during an awkward or uncomfortable moment, stay present and acknowledge the other person's discomfort. Follow up with a comforting phrase and an offer of support, rather than dismissing them and their feelings.[8] This simple act, whether you feel the same or not, validates your colleague's emotional state. Likewise, it is equally important to share in the happy and proud moments colleagues experience. Showing genuine happiness, support, and pride in a colleague's success reinforces the notion that success and achievement are not limited in quantity. Celebrating achievements strengthens teams, promotes creativity, and lifts entire departments.

> *Do the practice:* This is a practice that will strengthen your empathetic skills toward people with whom you disagree. It is common to occasionally be at odds with co-workers, patrons, acquaintances and family members. Personality conflicts and disagreements are part of any human life. Responding with curiosity and empathy rather than disdain creates an opportunity to better understand others and results in improved workplace interactions.
>
> Think of a colleague with whom you have experienced conflict. Consider what it would be like to be that person. What are the circumstances in their personal life that may be affecting their professional behavior? Are they experiencing family trauma, sleep deprivation, grief, or going through a divorce? What known or hidden health concerns may be playing a role in their behavior?
>
> How does this person act during difficult moments in the workplace? Do they withdraw, become aggressive, play the victim, or are they the hero of their own stories? How might workplace dynamics such as incivility, bullying, punishing the creative, gaslighting, or demanding workloads influence the interactions you have experienced with this colleague?
>
> Next, reflect on the positive interactions you have experienced with this person. Are there moments of authentic connection you have shared? Do you know or can you infer what makes this colleague happy at work? What do they most like to do?

After considering your colleague's challenges, reactions, and perspectives, how might you respond the next time feelings of contempt or irritation arise during an interaction with them? How might you go about building a better relationship with them?

Case study: Reference desk supervisor Andre recently arranged for himself and several of his colleagues to attend a two-hour off-site training during one of the busiest times of the year for their organization. He was certain this training about workplace communication would give him and his colleagues a deeper understanding about some of the interpersonal aspects of their work and allow them to give better customer service regardless of departmental affiliation in the workplace. The team he assembled for training included two librarians from his reference department, three staff members from the service desk who were required to attend this training, and two staff members from technical services who were rarely invited to participate in professional development training. In total, about one-third of the library staff would attend the training. About a week before the training course, the library director called Andre into her office to tell him that he could only bring his reference employees to the training. Andre thought the decision might be because the training would leave the library understaffed for several hours, but he thought the employees who were covering were happy to do so.

Andre was disappointed by the news that only librarians were to attend the training. He knew the technical services employees were looking forward to receiving the training, and Andre himself thought that everyone would benefit from the opportunity. It was important to him personally that all employees receive regular training, and the wider the scope, the better it was, as far as he was concerned. He thought that professional development made everyone feel valued, and by canceling the training for some but not all employees, he thought the staff members would feel devalued and disheartened. After the email went out about the training cancellation, George, one of the technical services staff members, stopped by Andre's office. George was visibly upset by the news and mentioned that he had been looking forward to getting away from his desk and learning something new for the first time in a while.

Reflection

In the extended practice of Empathetic Reflection and Action, you will more deeply engage in Mindful Practice as you consciously reflect on your assumptions about other people, your assumptions about situations at your workplace, and assumptions about your own decisions and actions in the workplace. Stephen Brookfield refers to this process of mindfully reflecting on your thoughts and actions in order to improve your skills as a critically reflective teacher as "hunting assumptions."[9] We know from experience that hunting assumptions, whether for teaching or everyday life, is not an easy or comfortable process. Michelle Reale notes that the process of reflection requires honesty in your reflections, a healthy non-attachment to your own ego, and acknowledgment that your confidence may take a bruising in the process.[10] Begin the process by assuming that at least one of your long-held assumptions in the workplace might just be wrong. Honing your reflective skills with the activities in chapters 1–3 will prepare you for this section.

When hunting assumptions in the workplace for this 360 Librarian ideal, there are up to four elements of reflection for each interaction. The four elements of reflection for Empathetic Reflection and Action are

1. the context of the other person's knowledge about the situation;
2. the other person's interaction frame;
3. your own interaction frame; and
4. your intention to act.

Altogether, these active and immediate practices for librarians clarify your assumptions and expectations during any interaction and allow for mindful empathetic engagement in each moment.[11] As you reflect on these four elements, remember that all the biases, hierarchies, and power dynamics of larger social structures are also present within smaller arenas, such as classrooms, department meetings, and libraries.[12] Consider your own biases, power, and privilege by completing the *Do the practice* in the "Action" section in this chapter and actively work to dismantle injustices during your practice of this ideal.

When you reflect on the context of the other person's knowledge about the situation, check your assumptions about their attitude, reasons for engagement, and definition of success. For instance, a student who has been required to seek your counsel may appear or be more nervous or discontented than one who finds you on their own. Regardless, both students would agree that learning how to get good sources at the library is a successful outcome. A colleague who needs your approval for a project might approach you with a different attitude than one who invites you to lunch, though not always. Two of your colleagues could approach you with complaints, but the complaint about the noise level in the shared office may have a much different tenor and outcome than the complaint about weekend safety measures. Knowing more about the context of the situation, as well as the other person's perception of the situation, will help you react in a more appropriate manner.

> *Do the practice:* Think about an extended interaction you had with someone during your day. What was their atti-

tude like when they first greeted you? What was it like as they continued to interact with you? Did it change based on your responses? Why did this person approach you? Were they required to seek you out? Did they know why they were interacting with you in particular or could anyone have helped them? Could that have affected their attitude? What was their definition of success for this interaction? Did they need information? Direction? Collaboration? Did you help them achieve that success, or help them find someone who could achieve that success with them?

When you reflect on the other person's interaction frame, you are trying to find out more about their background, how they typically collaborate with others, and what they think about you. You are finding out the context of the person in front of you, regardless of the situation. This can be assessed through observation of their verbal and visual cues, through direct questions, or through your own firsthand knowledge of the other person. Characteristics we consciously or subconsciously consider during an interaction may include: Is this person in a position perceived as superior, inferior, or on equal footing as myself? What is this person's education level? How does it compare to mine? With what expectations does this person enter our conversation? As we try to make sense of the world around us, we make assumptions and judgments about those with whom we interact all the time. As 360 Librarians have a continual practice of mindfully and nonjudgmentally interacting with the world, these automatic assumptions and judgments of others will decrease as your practice increases. Furthermore, assessing these kinds of dynamics will shed light on the inherent power structures within the library,[13] giving you a chance to identify and dismantle unfair structures.

Do the practice: At least once a day, without pre-judging the person in front of you, try to be more aware of someone else's interaction frame. Ask more questions about the knowledge they already bring to the interaction. Find out about their understanding and expectations of you, given your position in the library. Without doing their work for them, work within this other person's interaction frame instead of your own.

When you reflect on your own interaction frame, you may begin to feel more certain of your answers. You may think you know your own mind. With reflection, though, you will perceive more layers of meaning. In addition to your knowledge of your background with the situation and your default collaboration style, you also bring your history of successes and failures in your career as well as your entire self-identity into your interaction frame. This happens whether you realize it or not. Brookfield writes that we must interrogate our "autobiographies of teachers and learners" to become more reflective in the classroom,[14] and the same is true for all interactions in the workplace.

We often have blind spots when performing critical self-reflection. In an effort to remove the blinders, think about the hierarchical or administrative structure that influences your interactions and outcomes. Question the assumptions you hold that reinforce the power of the hierarchy or administration, even—or especially—if you are part of the administration. What choices do you make simply because you're in power? Do you do some things because they've always been done that way? Are you making decisions paternalistically? Some librarians might feel that because they are public servants they are naturally perceived to be altruistic or trustworthy or honorable and they make benevolent decisions for their patrons or employees based on those perceptions. But all humans hold different opinions and perceptions of situations and other people based on their interaction frame and knowledge of the situation. Some may perceive all librarians, even you, as overbearing or untrustworthy or over-educated snobs. In order to find out, you have to ask or intuit their attitudes. Forthrightly exploring these relationship dynamics "is often the first step in working more democratically and cooperatively with students [patrons] and colleagues."[15]

> *Do the practice:* Answer the questions above: What choices do you make simply because you're in a position of power? If you are at a service desk, you hold power over your patrons, so consider the little things you do every day. Do you do some things because they've always been done that way? Are you making decisions paternalistically?

The fourth element of reflection is your intention to act. This is a quick reflection in order for you to align the options available to you with a knowledge of the pathways you might take to success. It includes understanding and combining your perception of the other person's knowledge and desires, your own expertise, and your responsibilities in the workplace. It may include some questions to understand the expectations of others. Try not to get overwhelmed by the choices available to you during this reflection; let empathy for others and yourself be your guide. Consider which pathway might help the other person achieve greater agency or control over their own interests and actions while also help you achieve your own goals.

Do the practice: The next time you are at a decision point, stop. Check your perceptions. Are you operating firmly within the other person's interaction frame? Have you considered any rote actions because you're in a position of power? What is the preferred outcome of the interaction for the other person? Is there a way for you to incorporate this outcome into your decision-making process?

Taken together, the four reflections gather information about the situation and the perceptions and contexts of everyone involved in an interaction in the workplace. The reflections can happen in the moment or may be completed before or after a meeting or any critical incident in the workplace. If you need to, ask for more time to reflect on difficult circumstances, but take care not to use reflection as a stalling technique or a method to control the outcome of a workplace decision.

Case study, continued: As he went about his day, Andre couldn't help but return to his interaction with George. He felt that by simply communicating the decisions of his superiors to George and the others, he was perpetuating a message that staff members were inferior to librarians and not essential to the library's infrastructure. For Andre, this was not in line with his egalitarian ideals. He sensed that George and his other colleagues were not just disappointed in the decision but were feeling defeated at their place in the organization. Andre remembered his last job when he was part of the support staff and recalled the instances in which he felt expendable. He didn't want his colleagues feeling that way, so he decided to go back to the library director to advocate for training the staff as well as the librarians.

Action

Human agency, or the ability of each individual to act according to their own needs, desires, and beliefs is the crux of Empathetic Reflection and Action. In a 360 Librarian's practice, we understand that as part of an organization that provides access to materials via a proxy, firewall, or other gateway, we should actively create moments of agency with others as much as possible. In stepping back from our places of power, we work with others so they may step forward to empower themselves. Stepping back, especially with kindness, empathy, and respect for the knowledge of others, completes the process of Empathetic Reflection and Action.

As a rallying cry of resistance and empowerment, human agency is—or should be—a fundamental driver of social change. Studies and theories from a wide variety of disciplines, including economics, psychology, sociology, and education, position agency as one essential dimension of well-being.[16] In libraries and information literacy instruction, critical pedagogy dismantles the power structures of learning and creates moments of agency for students in the classroom. This requires instruction librarians to turn away from the idea of librarians as lecturing experts, de-center themselves from instruction, and democratically work with the students to create new knowledge in the classroom.[17]

Decentering yourself from the organizational power structure can sometimes cause a conscious or unconscious rise in your ego-response. The ego, while often thought of as a sense of pride in oneself, is much more complex in practice. The ego is what gives humans their sense of personal identity. From birth, we are socialized to create an identity for ourselves. This self-created identity comes from labels we have created for ourselves or labels from others that we have accepted.[18] Over time, our ego dictates how we perceive, interact with, and respond to the people around us. Internalized "me first" or "in my opinion" responses to highly charged situations become automatic and are often ineffective. Even in mundane interactions, it can be difficult to quiet the ego-response, focus on the other person, and allow the other person space to give information, request assistance, explore new ideas, or do whatever they need to do with you as their social partner.

If you are in a workplace where you do not feel you have the agency to act on your own or others' behalf, turn this ideal on its head to advocate for yourself. First, try the practices in this section to establish your reflective knowledge base about your own agency and the agency of those around you. Then, use the Reflection practices earlier in the chapter to infer the context of situations, interaction frames, and actions of yourself and others in your workplace. Then, as you feel more grounded in your own moments of agency, open yourself to empathetic reflection about your colleagues and patrons. This may allow you to begin to notice moments where you can position yourself to advocate more directly on your own or your patrons' behalf.

> *Do the practice*: Reflect on your own agency in the workplace. What positions of power, in official or unofficial capacities, do you hold? What decisions, small or large, do you make that affect the entire organization? Do you usually create your own daily calendar or task list? How does that act, or lack thereof, affect your ability or inclination to positively interact with others?
>
> Reflect on your colleagues' agency. Are they able to make their own decisions or influence the direction of your organization? Are there "fiefdoms" within your organization,

the grasping control of which belies a feeling of inadequacy or fear? Or do your colleagues work together for the greater good of your organization?

Reflect on your patrons' agency. Why do they seek you out? Do they know about the services and resources you offer? Do they know how to use your services and resources, or do they have to seek out you or your colleagues for assistance? Do you possess services or resources they cannot otherwise afford? Is there a gatekeeper for resources? How might you make access to these resources easier for your patrons?

Do the practice: Think about a moment when the power or agency shifted in an interaction you have had during the workday or in your personal life. Who drove this shift? Was it organic or did it seem like someone "took over" the situation? Maybe you stepped back and verbally or nonverbally invited a patron or colleague to drive the interaction. Or maybe, they stepped up to drive the interaction, requiring you to step back. What happened? How did you feel? If you were interacting with a colleague, what happened afterward? If you were with a patron, what methods or words did you use to continue to provide superior customer service throughout the interaction?

Case study, continued: Andre's library director was open to discussing options for staff training. She agreed that this training would be good for all members of library staff, but her primary point of conflict was the number of employees who would be out of the library at once. Once he learned this, Andre asked if he could arrange for this training session in the library. That way, anyone who worked at the library could decide to attend for all or part of the session. Andre's director agreed, stating that she was glad that all the employees would have the option to attend, provided all service points were covered and all urgent tasks were completed.

Integrating Empathetic Reflection and Action

Integrating empathy, reflection, and action into your workday creates a mini-360 opportunity for personal and professional growth time and time again.

When you create the space to understand our colleagues' emotions rather than projecting your emotions during interactions, workplace relationships flourish. Realizing and reflecting on these improved relationships builds confidence in professional skills as well as the confidence to believe the professional goals you have set for yourself are attainable regardless of naysayers and obstructionists. When confidence is paired with action, professional goals are realized. Celebrating these goals brings the process full circle as relationships continue to improve and confidence is continually bolstered.

360 Librarians who practice Empathetic Reflection and Action as their core mindset are highly adaptable changemakers who react to situations with genuine selfless action. Pairing an intellectual understanding of the components of this ideal with a daily practice of introspection that has empathy, reflection, and action at its center brings the 360 Librarian to a deeper understanding of the ideal and results in a practice that is blended, intuitive, and remarkable in its profound realness.

ENDNOTES

1. Frans B. M. de Waal, "Putting the Altruism Back into Altruism: The Evolution of Empathy," *Annual Review of Psychology* 59, no. 1 (January 2008), https://doi.org/10.1146/annurev.psych.59.103006.093625.
2. Although affective and cognitive empathy are the two types of empathy most reliably discussed in popular science today, C. Daniel Batson identified up to eight phenomena that have been classified as empathy in scientific and philosophical literature. His descriptions of affective and cognitive empathy along with other phenomena were part of his careful unpacking of the various definitions of empathy in C. Daniel Batson, "These Things Called Empathy: Eight Related but Distinct Phenomena," in *The Social Neuroscience of Empathy*, eds. Jean Decety and William Ickes (Cambridge: MIT Press, 2009).
3. David Hume, David Fate Norton, and Mary J Norton, *A Treatise of Human Nature* (Oxford: Oxford University Press, 2000); Elaine Hatfield, John T. Cacioppo, and Richard L. Rapson, *Emotional Contagion* (New York: Cambridge University Press, 1994); Batson, "These Things Called Empathy."
4. Adam Smith and Knud Haakonssen, *The Theory of Moral Sentiments* (Cambridge, UK: Cambridge University Press, 2002); Batson, "These Things Called Empathy."
5. Kristin D. Neff, "Self-Compassion: An Alternative Conceptualization of a Healthy Attitude Toward Oneself," *Self and Identity* 2, no. 2 (2003), https://doi.org/10.1080/15298860309032.
6. Neel Burton, *Heaven and Hell: The Psychology of Emotions* (Oxford, England, UK: Acheron Press, 2015), 154.
7. Christina Carter, "Save Your Marriage While Raising a Compassionate Child," Greater Good, March 16, 2011, http://greatergood.berkeley.edu/raising_happiness/post/save_your_marriage_while_raising_a_compassionate_child.

8. Travis Bradberry and Jean Greaves, *Emotional Intelligence 2.0: The World's Most Popular Emotional Intelligence Test* (San Diego, CA: TalentSmart, 2009).
9. Stephen Brookfield, *Becoming a Critically Reflective Teacher*, 1st ed. (San Francisco: Jossey-Bass, 1995).
10. Michelle Reale, *Becoming a Reflective Librarian and Teacher: Strategies for Mindful Academic Practice* (Chicago: ALA Editions, 2017).
11. The four elements of reflection are influenced by two of Brookfield's four critically reflective "lenses" to help focus practice in the classroom. Brookfield's lenses are our autobiographies as teachers and learners, our students' eyes, our colleagues' experiences, and theoretical literature. Brookfield, *Becoming a Critically Reflective*, Chapter 2.
12. Brookfield, *Becoming a Critically Reflective*.
13. Ibid.
14. Ibid.
15. Ibid., 9.
16. Sabina Alkire, "Subjective Quantitative Studies of Human Agency," *Social Indicators Research* 74, no. 1 (October 2005).
17. Maria T. Accardi, Emily Drabinski, and Alana Kumbier, *Critical Library Instruction: Theories and Methods* (Duluth: Library Juice Press, 2010); Andrea Baer, "Critical Pedagogy, Critical Conversations: Expanding Dialogue About Critical Library Instruction Through the Lens of Composition and Rhetoric," *In the Library With the Lead Pipe* (December 7, 2016), http://www.inthelibrarywiththeleadpipe.org/2016/critical-conversations/.
18. Eckhart Tolle, *A New Earth: Awakening to Your Life's Purpose* (New York: Plume, 2006).

CHAPTER 5

Reassurance

Reassurance is the fifth 360 Librarian ideal. It is the intentional act of bolstering others' confidence through matched informality levels, appropriate and timely humor, and positive reinforcement using respectful and engaged communication, emotional intelligence, and mindfulness. It is also the act of bolstering your own confidence with reflective thinking and journaling, among other practices. In this chapter, we unpack the complexities of reassuring students, colleagues, and ourselves.

Taking an active role in bolstering another person's confidence is almost exclusively an externally focused act. 360 Librarians practicing this ideal vocalize positive communication with no expectation of feeling or feedback in return. This is not to say Reassurance is a hollow act of recitation, of rote playacting, nor should it leave the 360 Librarian in an emotional hole at the end of a day filled with reassurance. The positive reassurance that occurs via this ideal *must* be sensitive, genuine, and timely and offered in such a way that it feeds your own emotional, social, and professional well-being. Authentic relationships are forged when the disingenuous communication that results from competition and ego response is set aside. Meaningful interactions filled with reassuring words and actions genuinely contribute to patrons' and colleagues' achievements and the success of the organization's mission.

The Neuroscience and Competencies of Emotion

Increasingly, research supports that optimism and efficacy are the building blocks that bolster confidence in ourselves and others. This, in turn, results in the ability to deal with difficult situations and the courage to use our professional expertise for creative endeavors and solutions.[1] The idea that a simple reassuring word or a comfortable conversation can alter someone else's mindstate has a basis in neuroscience. As we have discussed in previous chapters, emotions are contagious. Goleman, Boyatzis, and McKee explain that our emotion centers are affected by our communication partners. During interpersonal communication, verbal or nonverbal, there is a kind of physiological intermingling between people that leads to changes in emotion. Scientists describe this phenomenon as "interpersonal limbic regulation."[2] The open-loop nature of the limbic system, a region in the brain responsible for emotion and behavior, among other things, explains why you laugh when those around you laugh, and why you might cry when you watch a sad movie. It also explains why so many rally and respond to others with compassion and empathy when a natural disaster strikes. The opposite is true for organ systems like the circulatory system, which is considered a "closed-loop" system.[3] What happens in the circulatory system of your family members or coworkers does not change your physiology. For example, the fact that your coworker, spouse, or partner has high blood pressure does not influence your blood pressure. What might influence your blood pressure is the emotional reaction you have to your coworker, spouse, or partner, and that happens via your limbic system. The interpersonal limbic regulation, or physiological intermingling, decides whether you'll have stress-related spikes in heart rate and blood pressure or a calming, meditative moment that slows your heart rate and lowers your blood pressure.

With the understanding that our words and actions can influence the people around us, Reassurance is a practice best developed alongside or after other 360 Librarian skills involving deep empathy. The empathetic skills of "sensing others' development needs" and "anticipating, recognizing, and meeting customers' needs" fall under Goleman's Social Competence section of the Emotional Competence Framework[4] and is practiced and discussed in all four other ideals as well. Empathy involves not only discerning and taking an active interest in another person's point of view but also constructively promoting and bolstering their need for developing and improving as a scholar or as a professional. The empathetic ability to discern the anxiety a patron is experiencing during a reference interview or the aloofness of a colleague is the basis for the social connection and understanding that is established with this ideal.

As in other ideals, empathy and compassion toward yourself and using positive reinforcement on your own actions is an important part of developing self-confidence. In Goleman's Personal Competence section of the Emotional Competence Framework, he defines self-confidence as "a strong sense of one's self-worth and capabilities,"[5] and notes that the absence of self-confidence often leads to crippling self-doubt.[6] Self-confidence can be an antidote to a work environment that is rife with negative behavior like bullying, obstructionism, gaslighting, scolding, or ostracization. Negative behavior like this is sometimes dismissed as politics but leads to a workplace culture that breeds fear of failure, a lack of productivity, a lack of creativity, and little to no motivation. In contrast, a cadre of self-confident people in an organization creates the space and opportunity to break from groupthink and provides an opportunity to present a view that doesn't fit the mainstream mold.[7] In addition, it provides space for authentic leadership while healing a toxic culture.

The Practice of Reassurance

We originally conceived of Reassurance as an expansion of the RUSA Reference Standard 5.0, Follow-up, which tasks the librarian with ensuring that the patron is satisfied with the reference interaction. As a 360 Librarian ideal, we propose that Reassurance is more than the last action in any interaction. It is a way to practice clear and engaged communication and establish an easy rapport with the people you meet throughout the day. The three methods of practice for Reassurance—deliberate informality, humor, and positive reinforcement—are all based on agile use of language and can be deployed as needed during the day or during a single encounter.

All three methods of Reassurance may—and should—be regularly used on yourself during the workday. Exercising self-compassion and self-acceptance using Reassurance trains the mind to accept imperfection and categorize a less-than-stellar interpersonal interaction as a one-time event.[8] Self-compassion, which is also a main component of the 360 ideals Mindful Practice and Emotional Awareness, creates positive emotions which enhance resilience and decrease stress and subsequently leads to greater overall confidence and competence in your career.[9]

Deliberate informality

The first method of Reassurance, deliberate informality, is the act of adjusting your speech patterns and body language to match your conversational partner. As with Engaged Communication, subtly mirroring the patron's speech patterns shifts the power dynamic to place patron and librarian on equal footing during the interaction.[10] Removing hierarchical status through speech establishes a base-level rapport upon which to build a more long-lasting relationship. In the case of a single reference encounter, a genuine practice of deliberate informality allows the patron to be encouraged by familiar speech.

Paralanguage, as we briefly visited in chapter 3, Engaged Communication, consists of vocalizations that accompany speech, such as volume, stressing parts of a sentence, the pitch and rate at which someone speaks, rhythm, and the use of pauses.[11] Paralanguage research pioneer George Trager developed a paralanguage classification system consisting of *voice set,* or the context in which the speaker is communicating, which includes characteristics such as culture, age, gender and mood; *voice qualities* comprised of volume, pitch, articulation, rhythm, and accent; *vocalizations* that express emotion during speech; *vocal qualifiers* that define how the message is communicated, such as yelling, scolding, or speaking with a lilt in the voice; and *vocal segregates,* or the ums and uhs that reinforce the listener is following along and help to regulate the dialogue.[12] The ability to be cognizant and discerning of each of these elements is key during an attempt to match formality levels with colleagues and patrons. For instance, matching the mood, pitch, and volume of your answers to a patron's question will quickly establish rapport by affirming their general mien. Then, matching emotion and using similar filler phrases like a "mmm" to indicate listening that matches your patron's "mmm?" question phrase will ensure comfort and continued compatibility during the conversation.

For libraries, much of the research surrounding deliberate informality is in the area of virtual reference, or chat reference. In multiple large-scale studies of chat transcripts, several researchers found that librarians typically used slang, contractions, emoticons, lower-case letters, or punctuation to lower formality levels. Librarians also disclosed their own lack of knowledge or confusion to the patron to create rapport and lower the formality level. This lower formality afforded the patrons the ability to save face in the act of asking for help.[13] Saving face, or preserving one's own status or social role in a positive manner,[14] requires what Lynn Westbrook describes as a "dance" of formality levels for both librarian and patron during chat reference interactions. In Westbrook's study, most librarians held a slightly higher formality level than their patron but tended to raise and lower the formality to match that of their patron during the interaction.[15]

360 Librarians who mirror or adjust their formality levels with ease understand that sometimes a high level of professionalism is called for during serious situations like handling a crisis, a complaint, or unruly behavior. Language and de-escalation skills used with a patron who displays behaviors stemming from a mental illness may vary dramatically from the language and de-escalation skills used for an upset parent or an irate university professor. The genuineness of an interaction with matched formality levels is the key to positive reassurance. Mirroring formality levels does not require overtly mimicked speech patterns or the use of unfamiliar slang. Suddenly adopting a patois or using culturally specific phrases simply to try to match your interaction partner's speech or culture is insensitive at best and offensive at worst. Instead, a natural smile to match theirs along with a "Hey, how's it going?" to match their "Hiya!" works well to make them feel welcome and comfortable.

Do the practice: When interacting with a patron who has a complaint, consider the communication barriers that might hinder matching formality levels. Respond to some of these questions in your 360 Journal:

1. **Prejudging:** Are you prejudging the patron based on their social status, education level, or physical appearance? Is this patron a frequent complainer? If so, does that influence whether or not you attempt to match formalities?

2. **Power:** Are you in a position of power? If so, how does that influence how you interact or respond? Is there a power struggle occurring between you and the patron? If so, how does this affect your interactions? If you set aside your ego responses during a power struggle, how might that influence the interaction?

3. **Language:** Do you knowingly (or unknowingly) use library jargon rather than the patron's vernacular? If so, how does the patron respond? How can you match formalities if a patron is not a native English speaker or communicates using sign language or through other nonverbal means?

4. **Listening and reacting:** Are you truly listening to the patron and their complaint or are you formulating your answer in your head as they talk? Are you taking their complaint seriously or are you giving them lip-service? How can you respond to patrons so they feel like they are being heard and their needs are accommodated?

Do the practice: If you monitor chat reference at your library, take care to reassure patrons by lowering your formality level. Use emoticons every so often, and describe your own difficulties with patrons who seem to be most confused. Use more exclamation points and fewer periods, and don't be afraid of incomplete sentences. Empathetically engage with chat patrons as much as you would with those in front of you.

Case study: Linda, an early-career librarian with only a few years of teaching behind her, was at the end of a full week of instruction sessions at her large university library. As she walked into her last class of the day and began her usual round of welcoming and chatting with the students in the classroom, she noticed one student in the back of the room with her head down. After walking over, Linda realized this student had a session with her in a different class last week. She welcomed her back to the library and asked if she would move closer to the front of the room so she could work with others during the lesson to come. The student raised her head and sighed. "I just had this class last week," she said. "I understood everything then. I know it all and I don't need to go over it again. I'm just here for the attendance points." Linda was taken aback and momentarily at a loss for words. She never had someone admit that to her before, although she often had her suspicions that students were working through moments of boredom during class sometimes. As she quickly reflected on how to respond, Linda knew that responding from her position of power and demanding that this student follow her instructions and participate in class would probably backfire. Other students in the room were now watching the interaction, so she was careful to contain her shock over this student's words, set aside her immediate feelings of offense and anger, and instead continue to engage the student on her terms. "Aw, that's understandable," she said. "A lot of classes come through here at the same time. Luckily, we tweak what we teach for different classes, so we'll build on what you already know."

Humor

The second method of Reassurance, humor, can relieve anxiety, promote a less formal view of library services, and build rapport with patrons.[16] Typically, "humor" is thought of as jokes or one-liners that evoke lighthearted laughter from an audience or a social interaction. When used for reassurance, we look to Joshua J. Vossler and Scott Sheidlower's definition of humor to include "any technique that demonstrates a warm, friendly personality or that reveals yourself to [others] in a way that makes them feel closer to you."[17] In other words, your proclivity toward putting social partners at ease in any given environment, whether or not there is laughter, can be seen as humor. With that in mind, it is important to note at the outset that humor that is sarcastic, insulting, culturally specific, or otherwise alienating should always be avoided.[18]

The use of humor creates an informal air that quickly establishes a positive atmosphere. For example, the use of self-deprecating humor can be seen as a way to empathize with a beleaguered patron or colleague and create the impression of an even playing field by removing the power differences inherent in professional and patron/librarian relationships.[19] In addition, research suggests that the use of humor lessens stress and anxiety.[20] In the classroom, even cracking an old, stale joke before an instruction session is a common public speaking technique that lightens the mood and creates rapport.

Humor in professional settings, especially self-deprecating humor, does create some vulnerability and therefore is often met with resistance. The use of affiliative humor, such as a humorous anecdote or an inside joke, is a less vulnerable option than self-deprecating humor and is often seen as a non-threatening attempt to enhance conversation and build rapport. It also evens out status levels and reduces the social distance between communication partners.[21]

> *Do the practice:* Incorporating humor can be as simple as mindfully acknowledging the mood during an interaction at the reference desk, during an instruction session, or while interacting with colleagues during a meeting. Is it relaxed and loose or tense and terse? Begin by mindfully setting the intention to enter social interactions with humor, remembering that humor can be defined as simply as a warm friendly demeanor that puts others at ease. Next, take a moment to be emotionally aware of your patron's or colleague's mood. Consider the interaction and decide on the best type of humor to use. Would self-deprecating humor, a one-liner, or affiliative humor be most conducive to the situation? Observe colleagues who naturally incorporate humor into their interactions. Reflect on their techniques. Are there any techniques that you can incorporate into your daily interactions?

Case study, continued: When the student sighed again and started slowly moving to another seat, Linda knew she only partially won her over. Other students were noticing this student's attitude and it seemed to be affecting the tone of the class before she even started. Linda knew that she needed to lighten the mood a little before beginning her lesson. For her, this meant keeping a positive attitude and using a little self-deprecating humor to align herself with the class. "Okay, y'all," she said, "some people call librarians superheroes because we know all the super-secret ways to get to articles quickly. I'm *totally* not a superhero, I can tell you that, but I definitely wouldn't mind a sidekick or two in class today. Who's been here before or has used the library?" A few students raised their hands around the room, including the student who attended class the week before. "Awesome! I'm looking to you to help me out. That way, by the end of class today, everyone will possess research superpowers!"

Positive reinforcement

The third method of Reassurance, positive reinforcement, is the act of giving voice to encouraging comments in order to overcome the internal negative voice of the patron or colleague. We believe that words have power and these small phrases that may seem pithy or unimportant to librarians will resonate with stressed and overworked students and colleagues. Positive reinforcement that may contradict the "code of ethics" ideal of reserving judgment about a reference question or might seem odd in the context of a professional relationship is often vital in the service of reassurance and rapport-building.[22] Professionals who are adept at the ideal of Emotional Awareness recognize the emotions in themselves and others during interactions that call for rapport and reassurance and work to create a positive experience for everyone involved.

Psychologists report that human nature has a "negativity bias" woven into it from infancy. Despite the fact that most of the events we experience are neutral or positive, we are greatly affected by and tend to have vivid memories of negative experiences.[23] Consequently, when we forget to engage in positive, self-affirming, compassionate thoughts, it is easy to revert to defensive routines such as negative self-talk to cope when we are ill at ease. This behavior undermines our ability to produce positive results, writes Richard Boyatzis and Annie McKee. As negativity and hopeless feelings begin to surface, decisions are often made based on irrational musings rather than reality because these negative feelings affect our perceptions of ourselves and our environment.[24] Positivity can retrain the mind to notice and retain neutral or positive experiences, which then leads to neutral or positive self-talk, creative solutions, and mindful awareness of the environment at large.[25]

The ability to sense when students and colleagues are feeling inadequate and subsequently taking an active interest in bolstering their confidence with positive, reassuring comments can inspire them to see potential in themselves that they may not have been able to internalize prior to a positive, reassuring interaction, notes Maria Gonzalez. Positive, reassuring behavior "exude[s] an energy that captures the imaginations of those you lead and serve, and you inspire them to aspire to achieve great things."[26]

To build relationships with your students using positive reinforcement, first disrupt the negativity bias and any associated negative internal chatter both they and you may possess about your interactions at the library. For instance, when a student displays emotions that bubble up due to severe library or research anxiety, actively seek avenues to bolster their confidence and create a positive association with the library. You might first match formalities in an effort to even the playing field between you and the patron, then offer empathetic, reassuring comments such as, "I can understand your confusion. There are so many databases to choose from!" "I'm happy to walk you through a few database searches so you will feel more comfortable searching on your own," or "Once you do a few searches, you'll feel like an old pro."

> *Do the practice:* Think about your interactions with your patrons. Are they generally positive or negative?
>
> If you perceive most of the interactions as positive, think of ways to continue these positive interactions. Can you offer a physical item like a branded bookmark to your community patrons that affirms your great community? Reinforce your belief in the success of your students by telling them you know they'll do a great job on their assignment. Record and remember the positive interactions in your 360 Journal.
>
> If you perceive most of the interactions as negative, how can you employ some of the Mindful Practice ideas in chapter 1 to interrupt the negativity bias you carry when you're working with them? Brainstorm your best methods in your 360 Journal.

Building a culture of positivity within the workplace is beneficial to creating strong interpersonal connections with colleagues. Much like the Harvard study we mentioned in chapter 1, Mindful Practice, a study conducted by Diener and Seligman concluded that building and maintaining strong, authentic, trusting relationships is key to happiness and positivity.[27] When stronger connections are forged, organizational psychologist Elizabeth Cabrera writes, people tend to have affirming perspectives of their colleagues. This creates an amicable atmosphere where personal growth, creativity, and motivation thrive. In addition, as the emotional support afforded within a culture of positivity leads to greater cooperation and less conflict among team members. Those who experience positive emotions such as joy, gratitude, hope, and inspiration tend to have higher motivation, make better decisions, are more creative and more productive. Cabrera encourages leaders to strategically build a culture of positivity by focusing on "respect and appreciation, recognition, trust and generosity," or the four elements of good relationships in the workplace. Simple strategies such as asking for opinions and ideas and then sincerely listening and acting on the suggestions; acknowledging innovative ideas, a positive demeanor, or a job well done; demonstrating trustworthiness and your trust for others; and acting from the center of a generous spirit creates workplace positivity where colleagues and patrons feel respected, encouraged, and empowered.[28]

> *Do the practice:* Reflect on your current relationships within your workplace. Think of your relationship with a colleague, a supervisor, someone who reports to you, or a patron you interact with on a regular basis. What small reassuring practices can you engage in to improve interpersonal relationships? Write a 360 Journal reflection based on the following questions.
>
> Think about opportunities to celebrate successes. How can the successful completion of a project be celebrated? Has there been a time when colleagues worked above and beyond expectations or completed a physically demanding task that falls outside of their normal job description? How was that celebrated? How could that be celebrated in the future? When someone shares complimentary comments about coworkers and staff, do you relay the message to those involved? Do you share heartfelt praise and recognition when you are pleased with a colleague's performance? How can you acknowledge your appreciation for the collegial relationships that have been forged within the workplace? Do you thank others for taking the first step to build bridges within the department?
>
> Acknowledging that success is not a finite commodity, how can you empower others to succeed? Can you create opportunities for employees to mentor others? When a temporary setback occurs in the department, how can you help others to focus on a solution rather than the problem? How can you recognize employees that truly embody authentic, generous, compassionate spirits? What rewards can be set in place to encourage others to embody the same spirit?

Positive reinforcement is one part of this ideal that must be practiced reflectively. It is the constant heartbeat of the entire 360 Librarian framework.

360 Librarians with the ability to reflect positively on their work, instead of just critically, will have better stamina and resiliency to see themselves through times of low morale. Regular reflection in your 360 Journal is a vital outlet for self-compassion and empathy and a practice that will ease rumination and anxiety about your day-to-day interactions.

> *Do the practice*: Keep your own positive reinforcement journal pages as part of your 360 Journal. Separate from calendars, annual review documents, or other day-to-day administratively stipulated documents, keep a series of pages that celebrates the positive feedback you have received. Designating one week per double-page spread, celebrate your successful activities each week. Be specific. Don't stint in your lavish praise of yourself. Attach letters of thanks and print out and keep inspiring emails. Set inspirational goals and share them or keep them secret, whichever is more comfortable for you. Either way, write them down in your 360 Journal and make a celebratory note each time you get closer to your goals.

Case study, continued: As she continued to talk to the students about what they could expect to learn from the next hour of instruction, Linda felt like the students in the room were more engaged and open to learning than a few minutes before. She assured them that they would be researching faster and more effectively with the tools and tips she would leave them with that day. She could tell her reluctant student was still a little unhappy, but Linda knew that she had to continue her session for the whole class to learn.

After the instruction session, Linda allowed herself to feel the emotions that she set aside during her interaction with the student before class. She was angry and offended that the student felt she "knew it all" when Linda herself learned new things at work all the time. She was frustrated that a student unsettled her during a time that she usually used to prepare herself mentally for the class to come. She was unsure whether or not she reacted to the situation appropriately, and knew she would replay the interaction in her head for weeks. To process, Linda decided to talk about the situation with her colleagues and learned that a few of them also had this situation happen to them. Together, they reflected on how to handle similar classroom issues. Linda's colleagues reassured her that while she can control a lot of what happens in the classroom, she is not responsible for a student's attitude or actions. Reflecting on the interaction, Linda wondered, what emotions and experiences were underlying this student's behavior? Was the student feeling ill? Was the student feeling stressed or anxious due to personal issues? Was the contentious exchange due to misplaced anger? Did library instruction sessions overwhelm the student? Linda concluded that the reason for the uncomfortable exchange, most likely, wasn't a personal attack. After this, Linda entered each instruction session with a curious, empathetic mindframe and with greater confidence in her ability to handle uncomfortable interpersonal exchanges.

Integrating Reassurance

For some 360 Librarians, deliberate informality, humor, and positive reinforcement do not feel natural or appropriate in the workplace. Their personalities are more reserved, their humor more dry, or their interactions with others relatively short or impersonal. If this is the case for you, first try a personal practice of self-reassurance, then open your practice to small moments of reassurance, and rest in the knowledge that small moments make a difference.

Other 360 Librarians are working in positions that afford them little power or agency and thereby what appears to be few opportunities for self-display in this manner. For people who feel they do not have agency in their workplace or for those who work in environments where bullying, micromanaging, or negativity is the norm, practicing this ideal takes a certain amount of trust in the practice. As the only person in the workplace reacting to situations with good humor or the only voice speaking positive affirmations, you may feel run down, vulnerable, or open to attack by workplace bullies. Continue your own practice without engaging these bullies, and recharge your positive energy through interactions with your patrons or outside of the workplace.

For others, the methods of Reassurance are completely intertwined with their personality. They are effusive with praise, always ready with a joke or two, and able to adapt to the formality of situations with relative ease. Those 360 Librarians would do well to practice Reassurance along with other 360 ideals in order to understand when and why to practice Reassurance in the most helpful manner. It can be a common problem for more extroverted people to inadvertently speak over or in place of quieter members of their organization or intimidate patrons with their enthusiasm. Use Reassurance, coupled with Mindful Practice and Engaged Communication, to heighten your awareness of others and find the best way to reassure yourself and others at work.

ENDNOTES

1. David L. Cooperrider and Diana Whitney, *Collaborating for Change: Appreciative Inquiry* (Williston, VT: Berrett-Koehler Publishers, 2000).

2. Daniel Goleman, Richard Boyatzis, and Annie McKee, *Primal Leadership: Unleashing the Power of Emotional Intelligence* (Boston: Harvard Business Review Press, 2013), 7. Goleman, Boyatzis, and McKee base this on Thomas Lewis, Fari Amini, and Richard Lannon's research in *A General Theory of Love* (New York: Random House).
3. Goleman, Richard Boyatzis, and Annie McKee, *Primal Leadership*.
4. Daniel Goleman, *Working with Emotional Intelligence* (New York: Bantam Books, 2000), 135.
5. Goleman, *Working with Emotional Intelligence*.
6. Ibid.
7. Ibid.
8. Deborah Schoeberlein David, *Mindful Teaching and Teaching Mindfulness: A Guide for Anyone Who Teaches Anything* (Somerville, MA: Wisdom Publications, 2009), 4.
9. Richard E. Boyatzis and Annie McKee, *Resonant Leadership: Renewing Yourself and Connecting with Others through Mindfulness, Hope, and Compassion* (Boston: Harvard Business School Press, 2005).
10. Matt Stock, "The Three R's: Rapport, Relationship, and Reference," *The Reference Librarian* 51, no. 1 (2009).
11. Alessandra Padula, "Paralanguage," in *Encyclopedia of Communication Theory*, eds. Stephen W. Littlejohn and Karen A. Foss (Los Angeles, CA: Sage, 2009).
12. George L. Trager, "Paralanguage: A First Approximation," *Studies in Linguistics* 13, no. 1–2 (1958).
13. Tammi M. Owens, "Communication, Face Saving, and Anxiety at an Academic Library's Virtual Reference Service," *Internet Reference Services Quarterly* 18, no. 2 (September 2013), https://doi.org/10.1080/10875301.2013.809043; Marie L. Radford, Gary P. Radford, Lynn Silipigni Connaway, and Jocelyn A. DeAngelis, "On Virtual Face-Work: An Ethnography of Communication Approach to a Live Chat Reference Interaction," *The Library Quarterly* 81, no. 4 (October 2011), https://doi.org/10.1086/661654; Lynn Westbrook, "Chat Reference Communication Patterns and Implications: Applying Politeness Theory," *Journal of Documentation* 63, no. 5 (2007), https://doi.org/10.1108/00220410710827736.
14. Erving Goffman, "On Face-Work: An Analysis of Ritual Elements in Social Interaction," *Psychiatry* 18, no. 3 (1955).
15. Westbrook, "Chat Reference Communication Patterns and Implications," 649–52.
16. Billie E. Walker, "Using Humor in Library Instruction," *Reference Services Review* 34, no. 1 (January 2006), https://doi.org/10.1108/00907320610648806; Marie L. Radford, "Encountering Virtual Users: A Qualitative Investigation of Interpersonal Communication in Chat Reference," *Journal of the American Society for Information Science and Technology* 57, no. 8 (June 2006).
17. Joshua J. Vossler and Scott Sheidlower, *Humor and Information Literacy: Practical Techniques for Library Instruction* (Santa Barbara, CA: Libraries Unlimited, 2011), xii.
18. Walker, "Using Humor in Library."
19. Vossler and Sheidlower, *Humor and Information Literacy*; Eric J. Romero and Kevin W. Cruthirds, "The Use of Humor in the Workplace," *Academy of Management Perspectives* 20, no. 2 (May 2006).

20. Walker, "Using Humor in Library"; Liz Bryson, "Humor Deficit: A Librarian's Guide to Being Funny and Competent," *Science & Technology Libraries* 28, no. 1–2 (August 2008), https://doi.org/10.1080/01942620802096978.
21. Romero and Cruthirds, "The Use of Humor."
22. Owens, "Communication, Face Saving."
23. Rick Hanson, *Buddha's Brain: The Practical Neuroscience of Happiness, Love, and Wisdom* (Oakland, CA: New Harbinger Publications, 2009); Amrisha Vaish, Tobias Grossmann, and Amanda Woodward, "Not All Emotions Are Created Equal: The Negativity Bias in Social-Emotional Development," *Psychological Bulletin* 134, no. 3 (2008), https://doi.org/10.1037/0033-2909.134.3.383.
24. Boyatzis and McKee, *Resonant Leadership*, 45.
25. Elizabeth F. Cabrera, "The Six Essentials of Workplace Positivity," *People & Strategy* 35, no. 1 (January 2012).
26. Maria Gonzalez, *Mindful Leadership: The 9 Ways to Self-Awareness, Transforming Yourself and Inspiring Others* (Mississauga, ON: Jossey-Bass, 2012), 153.
27. Ed Diener and Martin E.P. Seligman, "Very Happy People," *Psychological Science* 13, no. 1 (January 2002).
28. Cabrera, "The Six Essentials," 53–54.

PART 2

IMPLEMENTING AN INTENTIONAL 360 LIBRARIAN PRACTICE

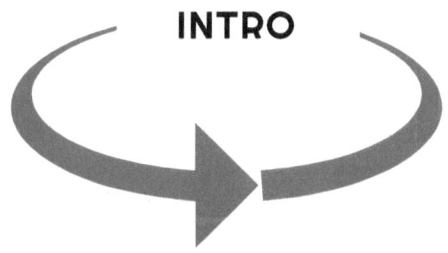

Introduction

Whether practiced by one person or an entire team, 360 Librarian ideals have a real effect on the workplace. A steadfast focus on mindfulness, emotional intelligence, and critical reflection creates a positive shift in workplace culture and allows for the space to form connections otherwise overlooked from day to day. 360 Librarians are sensitive to the everyday demands of library service and know that the practice of the five ideals of the 360 Framework establishes a roadmap for authenticity, resilience, and curiosity in the mind while reducing toxicity, judgment, and unhelpful criticism in the workplace.

The five steps of the 360 Framework are applicable to everyday situations as well as intermittent challenges in all areas of the library. So far, we have taken a deep dive into each ideal, examining the science and theory behind each and providing scenarios and practices to embody each step. Some chapters have further applications for specific roles in the library, while others are broader in scope. We have been encouraging readers to take the time to build new skills and internalize new habits, and because of this it may be some time since you first started your exploration of each ideal. This section will serve as a concise reminder of each ideal as it can be applied to various workplace situations.

In part II of this book, we focus on five specific domains in an academic library. In "360 Librarian Practice While Consulting with Students," we examine the interactions between librarians and their patrons. We step forward from traditional reference guidelines, providing advice on how to create authentic connections in even the briefest encounters. In "360 Librarian Practice in the Information Literacy Classroom," we align the 360 Librarian's classroom with the ACRL Framework in order to identify the mindful learning moment amid threshold concepts and active learning techniques. In "360 Librarian Practice in Reaching Out and Marketing the Library," we describe 360 Librarian outreach and marketing techniques that align spaces, resources, and programming to patron needs and share a few of our most exciting events and challenging situations. In "360 Librarian Practice in Working with Technology," we examine how to engage and disengage with technology mindfully and address emotional connections to technology in the workplace. In "360 Librarian Practice in Leading in the Library," we take another look at leadership techniques as they are practiced by the 360 Librarian. This time, we place particular focus on avoiding burnout while honing a reflective practice conducive to leading a cultural shift in the workplace. For each domain, we describe the philosophy and mindset as well as some actions of the engaged 360 Librarian.

In your domain, create a sustainable 360 Librarian practice by applying one or two ideals to your daily life. To begin, choose the ideal that feels the easiest to implement, like incorporating moments of mindful breathing throughout the day. Once that practice has been established, incorporate a second, such as reflective journaling about how mindful breathing has influenced your work life. Keep going to build your practice incrementally, using the exercises in this section of the book as your guide.

CHAPTER 6

360 Librarian Practice While Consulting with Students

For many researchers, the library is a comfortable place, but there are a significant number of people who experience library anxiety. Library anxiety includes a fear of libraries as a space as well as a feeling of being overwhelmed by the prospect of using library resources.[1] Researchers from all levels have varying degrees of proficiency and comfort with research, writing, and publishing, and 360 Librarians shouldn't assume the researcher's comfort or expertise with libraries and research.

In this chapter, we provide thought processes and actions to engage the anxious student during a reference encounter or a research consultation. We know that students who enter the library with a specific information need are typically operating under a high cognitive load before they begin their library research and can be anxious and unmoored before they venture to the reference desk or seek out a librarian for advice. Visibly anxious students require that librarians move beyond the linear script of easy reference and toward a learning environment full of empathy, communication, and plenty of reassurance. This breaks down traditional barriers and power structures between students and librarians, promotes an equitable partnership between students and the library, and ensures that anxious students feel comfortable navigating the library and its resources.

Mindful Practice

After some time at a reference desk, you might take simple reference transactions for granted. It is easy to lead students down comfortable research paths and rely on resources close at hand. It is more time-consuming and stressful to actively listen to a student's questions and meet them where they are, especially if they are having trouble articulating their information need. Mindful Practice allows you to discover and answer students' questions without judgment or bias regardless of your own internal or external distractions. By being fully present with the student, you'll demonstrate genuine interest, vastly reduce misunderstandings and judgment during the reference transaction, and allow the student to feel validated as they embark on their own research path. You might feel some anxiety as you move beyond your well-established comfort zones during reference interactions, but the positive impact on student success and your own increased confidence in your professional skills are worth the passing fear.

Embedded 360 Consulting Exercises

To suspend judgment when meeting with a student, begin by taking a moment to center yourself. On the breath in, set the intention to greet the researcher with curiosity. On the breath out, set the intention to suspend judgment. As you interact with the student, observe their nonverbal communication. Is there a sense of reluctance, anxiety, joy, or excitement? If you are sensing fear and reluctance to engage in the research process, be an emotional leader and proceed by offering reassurance. If you are sensing joy or excitement, match their emotional state while offering assistance. As you engage with the student, ask questions about their experience and comfort level with research, how they feel about embarking on this particular research project and how research makes them feel in general. Their responses will help you gauge their comfort level. Staying in the moment, engaging in conversation, and observing the student will provide an opportunity for you to influence and guide their emotional state.

Mindful Practice

Liz Chenevey

For me, mindfulness in both my personal and working life is all about breath. Through my practice of yoga, I have learned breathing and centering techniques that I carry with me beyond the mat and into the library. But often the most powerful technique for me is to simply take deep breaths in times of stress.

Anyone who has sat at a service desk knows the stress that can arise working with the public. My first academic library job was as a training coordinator and interim student supervisor for public services. For an introvert like me, being a public-facing staff member as well as a supervisor can often be draining. However, as a full-time staff member, I also had time away from the desk. I had an office where I could retreat to and breathe. I had breaks and would often use this time to practice walking meditation. My front-line staff was often at the desk for hours on end, without many opportunities to take a step away to refresh. This can lead to stressful or uncomfortable situations for staff and poor service interactions.

At my library, like many, we staff our front-line service points with students. Some of our students have worked in service jobs before, others are first-time workers with little experience working with the public. Compound that with the fact that the public is generally a group of their peers, friends even. Knowing this, I wanted to support our student staff in navigating how to provide professional service in a space that is also meant for them.

Inspired by my own mindfulness practice, I created a "Mindful Service Ethic" training for all desk staff. I wanted staff to go beyond the traditional idea of customer service and treat each desk interaction as its own unique opportunity to engage with our users. We aim our outreach to "meet students where they are," and I wanted our front-line services to reflect that. Beyond improving our service ethic, I wanted staff, especially our student workers, to be mindful of self-care in their work. To do this, I created what I called the "Mindful Service Loop" that took staff through the process of a desk interaction. This loop combined elements of the reference interview with mindfulness practices to help desk staff better meet users where they are and to practice self-care in that process. This "Mindful Service Loop" included steps typical in reference interviews such as "be approachable" and "communicate clearly" alongside mindful practices such as "validation," "active listening," "practicing self-care," and simply breathing. I made it clear to our students that if they were stressed, they could talk to supervisors and use opportunities to go behind the desk to take several calming breaths.

> My hope was that not only would the practice of mindful service improve user engagement but also improve our staff's confidence in their abilities, with the understanding that supervisors would support them in their self-care process.
>
> **Author Bio**
> *Liz Chenevey is the psychology librarian for James Madison University Libraries. She is interested in holistic public and instructional services and often incorporates mindfulness and social justice into her work. In her spare time, she enjoys walking, practicing yoga, gardening, and reading zines. She recently completed a 200-hour Yoga Teacher Training to further her own mindfulness practice and share it with her community.*

Emotional Awareness

To be adept at the ideal of Emotional Awareness during reference interactions, librarians should recognize emotions in themselves and others and work to create a positive experience for the patron. This can be accomplished by setting a positive emotional tone at the outset of the interaction. As mentioned in chapter 2, emotional contagion causes our emotions to shift, register, and sync with our conversational partner. Be an emotional leader during the reference transaction and practice equanimity while expressively transmitting positive feelings.

Many students enter libraries overwhelmed by the sheer amount of information that is available using the library's resources, are likely confused about how to access those resources, and may be concerned about their ability to determine the credibility of the information as they sift through their sources. They can't help but wonder if they have completed a thorough search or missed an important research study. Students with these feelings may show overt signs of anxiety or frustration. With all this in mind, be cognizant of how emotions influence the dynamics of the consultation or reference interaction.

Embedded 360 Consulting Exercises

Practice recognizing your emotions and the emotions of others. As a student approaches the desk for a consultation session, reflect on your current mood and the energy you are projecting. Have you just completed a successful research consultation that left you feeling satisfied? Have you just left a contentious department meeting that left you feeling depleted? Are you eager to help or eager to go home?

Next, take a moment to observe the student's verbal and nonverbal communication. Are they in a talkative state of confusion or excitement? What tone are they expressing with their verbal communication? What is their body language? Are they wringing their hands or looking at their feet? Is there any backchannel communication such as an exasperated sigh? What do you sense—frustration, confusion, friendliness, confidence?

Notice how the student's energy is influencing your energy. If you are in a somber mood as a bubbly student approaches, try to lighten your mood to match their mood. In doing so, notice whether the interaction left you feeling energized. If you are in a positive mood when an angry student approaches the desk, try to be an emotional leader and stay positive. Notice if this experience makes you feel edgy.

Knowing that it is important to be an emotional leader, take a deep breath and begin a confident inner dialogue that allows you to maintain equanimity during all interactions. Notice the physical sensations in your body when your mood is changing. Remind yourself that research and information-seeking are difficult and anything that happens during these interactions is not personal. Connect with the student on an emotional level, with compassion, and reassure them that their needs will be met.

After the consultation is completed, consider the original mood of the student as they entered the consultation session. How does that contrast with their mood as the consultation ended? What was your emotional state as the consultation ended? Why were you and your conversational partner feeling that way? Consider writing about this in a daily journal entry. Reflecting in this way may help you emotionally code shift more easily to become an emotional leader in difficult situations.

Engaged Communication

Building on Mindful Practice and Emotional Awareness, Engaged Communication is one way for librarians to influence how students think about information and the research process during a one-on-one research consultation. For us, the practice of Engaged Communication during a research consultation is often the most rewarding part of our day. During this time, we are fully able to express our passion and hold our students to a high standard of thinking and learning. We ask students questions they may not have thought about before. Rarely do we just give them what they ask for and let them leave. Using attentive two-way communication, we connect students with the resources at their disposal while conveying information literacy skills that can be used in a lifelong pursuit of credible knowledge. Engaged Communication consists of practicing a mindful presence, listening with focus, being responsive to feedback, and modeling authenticity.

Embedded 360 Consulting Exercises

When you meet with a student who has limited their scope of appropriate source material to online material, balance their information needs and expectations with a challenge to go beyond their typical scope. For instance, if the student demurs when you recommend books from your collection, explain the place and power of printed books in a research project. Ask them if they have used many books in their research before. If not, it could be because they are unfamiliar with how to read a book for research purposes and don't have the time to read many books cover to cover. Explain how to read parts of a book for research, and how to get the most out of a large body of scholarship. Always end your consultation with an offer to help them find the book on the shelf.

If the student appears to be using questionable source material for their project, ask where they first heard about their topic. Why do they take certain facts as truth? Have they explored what other experts in the field have to say about the topic? Do a quick exercise in fact-checking together to help them think more critically about their topic. Remember to use nonjudgmental language and ground the conversation in the idea of finding the best sources. With this same student, you may need to have a conversation about academic integrity. Ask them what makes a good source. Why would they want a friend to give them an unbiased version of something that happened when they weren't there? Why do they want to read reviews written by car experts, rather than a random person, when buying new tires for their car? Draw parallels to the act of finding and citing sources in a paper. Explain that it is important to find and use the best sources so their own argument is bolstered by experts in the field.

Empathetic Reflection and Action

Empathetic Reflection and Action during reference and consultation is the ability to reflect on the reference interaction as it happens, staying in tune with one's intuition regarding the student's information need and current state of mind and responding in a considerate and appropriate manner in light of these reflections. It requires a constant inner refrain of the four questions from chapter 4: In what type of learning context is the student operating? How might the student be framing this interaction? How am I framing this interaction? How can I offer agency to the student while assisting them with their information need? While you answer these four questions for yourself, you can recognize and clear the students' assumptions, adjust your own expectations, and engage mindfully with the student.

Embedded 360 Consulting Exercises

First, determine the student's learning context. What are they asking and why are they asking for it? Is this for a class or personal curiosity? Ask them about their history with the topic. Are they familiar with the terminology of their topic and of library research in general? If not, explain the jargon that surfaces throughout the interaction. Do they have experience with the library, and have they asked for help at the reference desk before? If not, explain library jargon and narrate your line of thinking and action as you search for source material together. Are they required to seek you out or have they found you on their own? Keep in mind that a forced interaction may be less successful, as the student may be reticent about receiving advice.

To find out how the student is framing the interaction, ask directly: What are their expectations? Do they expect you to give them the right answer, find the sources, or give advice about how to find information? The answer to this question allows you to immediately manage their expectations and frame your side of the interaction in a thoughtful, helpful manner.

As it is in all other areas of library service, the most important part of this ideal is a high degree of student agency as they learn how to satisfy their own information need. Throughout the reference interview or consultation, ask the student for clarification while you search and brainstorm answers to their questions. Teach them how to search for and analyze the information by modeling good questions and thinking aloud. Ask open-ended questions that allow students to take the lead in their own research projects.

Reassurance

When students begin a new research project, they can feel insecure or inadequate even if they have used the library successfully in the past. Your continual reassurance during a research consultation allows students to borrow your confidence and competence as you remind them of the research practice. Little by little, this reassurance chips away at fear and anxiety. In chapter 5, we described the practice of reassurance as a combination of deliberate informality, humor, and positive reinforcement. Reassurance of all kinds during a consultation session brings the 360 Librarian Framework full circle, as it encourages the student to see the consultation as the beginning of a useful relationship and turns the meeting into a positive learning opportunity for both student and librarian.

Embedded 360 Consulting Exercises

A genuine practice of informality affirms one's training and expertise as an information professional and allows the student to be comforted by familiar speech from someone in a position of power. There are several ways to practice deliberate informality, such as the use of less formal English, dropping library jargon for more common phrases, and making small talk to put the student at ease. Establish rapport by beginning the conversation with one of these informal icebreakers: "That is an interesting research question. I helped a student with a similar question last week," "I recently read an interesting article on that in the [insert title here]," "A colleague of mine is a big _____ fan. She would find this research question fascinating!" This small talk is less formal than stiff conversation about peer-reviewed articles and other overwhelming jargon-filled introductions to research methods. The student will also be relieved to hear that the research project is viable and others at the university share their interests.

Humor is an excellent antidote to anxiety. Poking fun at yourself for "being obsessed" about library search techniques or a particular subject matter gives students the opportunity to share your enthusiasm. Be real about your interests, though, as students will link your humanity to your interests and remember them (and you) in the future. A pop culture reference or a lighthearted joke about the weather allows students to think about something—anything—other than the tension they may feel about the reference encounter.

Once you acknowledge that the student is probably experiencing some degree of negative self-talk and insecurity as they approach the reference desk, you can begin to change that narrative with simple phrases of positive reinforcement. Try working the following phrases into the repertoire of small talk at the reference desk: "Wow, this is a challenging question. Thanks for bringing it here," "You've got a great start. Let's see what else we can find to dig a little deeper," and "This can be an overwhelming process. But you can do it! Let me teach you a few tricks to start out."

To continue to practice the reassurance ideal reflectively, you may choose to keep a physical or online notebook at hand, jotting down a few key elements of the interaction and, most importantly, cataloging the students' and your own emotional reactions. Answer these questions: What happened? What did I do? How did the student respond? How did this make me feel and/or react? How will I do things differently in the future?

ENDNOTES

1. Constance A. Mellon, "Library Anxiety: A Grounded Theory and Its Development," *College & Research Libraries* 47, no. 2 (1986), https://doi.org/10.5860/crl_47_02_160.

CHAPTER 7

360 Librarian Practice in the Information Literacy Classroom

The introduction of 360 Librarian ideals into the classroom is a natural extension of the personal practices developed in Part I of this book. In this chapter, we match 360 Librarian ideals to the frames in the Association of College & Research Libraries' *Framework for Information Literacy for Higher Education*.[1] For each ideal, we offer class exercises designed to challenge students to critically engage with information resources and develop ethical research practices. These exercises help students identify their own voice and agency, assume control over their own learning, and examine their reactions to and role in scholarly conversations.

The 360 Framework, like the ACRL *Framework*, is not intended to be incorporated in its entirety into every instruction interaction. Despite our best efforts, most library instruction still occurs in a single-class session or at a service desk. As a practicing 360 Librarian, you can imagine how overwhelming it would be for your students to apply all 360 Librarian ideals in under an hour. Approaching research in a mindful and critical manner can carry a high cognitive load, so think of the 360 Framework in the classroom as a guide to help students through the emotionally charged processes of research. Select one or two ideals that complement the instruction need and the learner best and develop your lesson plan around those ideals.

Creating contemplative learning moments infused with mindfulness, emotional intelligence, and critical reflection reinforces an individual practice for the instructor and encourages students to travel linked pathways to deeper understanding through research.[2] Introducing students to research as a mindful practice gives them introspective modes of inquiry that can lead to a more egalitarian worldview. Introspective modes of inquiry can also be used to combat confirmation bias and lead to a greater sense of connection and compassion with people who have opposing viewpoints. Embedding the 360 Framework into the research process initiates the reflection necessary to understand individual and collective roles in the scholarly conversation. Once these tools are practiced in the classroom, students can use these same tools outside of the classroom to examine information resources in everyday situations.

Mindful Practice

Mindful Practice in the classroom encourages students to stay on task, place a gentle focus on their research, and complete their research in a nonjudgmental manner. This ideal maps to the ACRL frames Authority is Constructed and Contextual and Research as Inquiry, both of which include dispositions related to the open-minded exploration and critique of source material.

Embedded 360 Learning Exercises

1. **What Do You Know?** This exercise of mindful writing allows students time to reflect and record everything they know about their research topic before beginning their research. It centers their mind on their topic and reminds them why they chose the topic. After the exercise, students should be able to articulate their blind spots more clearly and acknowledge their spheres of influence.
    - (10 minutes) For this exercise, have students open a new document on their laptops or get out a fresh sheet of paper. Announce to the class that you will be doing a series of one-minute writing exercises to better understand their assignment and their topics before beginning their search for information. Allow one minute of writing for each question set.
        - o Question set 1: What is the assignment? Why are you completing this assignment? What do you think the teacher wants you to learn as a result of this assignment?

- - Question set 2: What is your topic? Why did you choose this topic?
  - Question set 3: What do you already know about this topic? Where did you get that information? What is your opinion about this topic?
  - Question set 4: How might your political views, religious views, social class, and level of education contribute to your knowledge of and opinion about this topic?
  - Question set 5: How would someone of different political views, religious views, social class, or level of education feel this about this topic? Why?
- (15 minutes) After students complete the last question set, ask them why it is important for them to reflect on each question set in turn. For example, you might ask, "Why should you be able to articulate what your teacher wants you to learn as a result of this assignment?" Regardless of the answer, thinking about the question begins to turn students' minds toward the act of researching and writing.
- (5–10 minutes) If the class seems willing, ask students to share their mindful writing answers to see how other students perceive the same or similar topics.

2. **What Do the Experts Know?** This exercise offers students a chance to nonjudgmentally but critically engage with experts in their field at the beginning of their research journey. After completing this exercise, students will be able to objectively analyze research for expertise, spheres of influence, biased language, and an author's conclusions, and then objectively compare and contrast the authors' findings and their own worldview.
   - (10 minutes) Hand out copies of a short but scholarly opinion or editorial article relating to the course material. Each student should quickly skim the article. After skimming the article in groups of four, students should
     - circle language that indicates the author's expertise;
     - underline language that illuminates spheres of influence, background, or bias; and
     - star sections that contain the author's conclusions.
   - (5 minutes) In your groups, discuss how this author aligns with or differs from their knowledge or beliefs.
   - (5 minutes) As a class, report back. What are the author's expertise, bias, and conclusions? Does this fit into your own worldview or experience? Why or why not?
   - (5 minutes) Class discussion. Some questions to pose to the entire class may include: What is an expert? Are experts always right? What could make an expert wrong or not appropriate to use as a source?

Emotional Awareness

This 360 Librarian ideal develops emotional intelligence in the classroom. Students using this ideal work toward a calm and positive state for themselves and others while doing research. Mapping to the ACRL frames Scholarship as Conversation and Information Creation as Process, exercises using Emotional Awareness ask students to first consider their own emotional state and attachment to their research topics, then consider the emotions, attitudes, and potential biases of other people who create and consume information.

Embedded 360 Learning Exercises

1. **What's Your Emotional State?** Discussing library anxiety as a phenomenon with research students can help researchers name what they are experiencing, understand that they are not alone in this experience, and allow them to create a plan to alleviate the anxiety.
    - (3 minutes) Introduce library anxiety as a phenomenon. Share Constance Mellon's insights about students' feelings of confusion, shame, and fear during library research. Specifically, consider sharing this quote: "Confusion about using the library was reflected over and over in the journal entries, leading to a theory of library anxiety: students become so anxious about having to gather information in a library for their research paper that they are unable to approach the problem logically or effectively. The basis of library anxiety is that students' fears are due to a feeling that other students are competent at library use while they alone are incompetent, this lack of competence is somehow shameful and must be kept hidden, and asking questions reveals their inadequacies."[3] In addition, share an anecdote about a time that you were nervous or anxious when you were learning something new. Ask students to raise their hand if they ever felt a little unsure when learning new things.
    - (3 minutes) Invite students to take three minutes to write down all the feelings that surface when they are assigned a research project, as they begin searching for a topic to research, as they begin gathering resources, and so on. Tell them to write down any feelings they or someone else might typically experience while going through the research process.
    - (5 minutes) Share these feelings with a small group of four or five students. Remind them that these could be personal feelings or feelings they think someone else might have. This is a no-judgment zone! List on a single sheet the feelings that are shared among the members of the group and note any that are spectacular or unique.

- (5 minutes) Construct a class list of library-related emotions on a whiteboard. Ask the class how creating a mindful list and naming the emotions you and your colleagues are experiencing change their view of research.
- (5 minutes) As a class, enumerate three strategies for relieving stressful emotions related to the research process.

2. **What is Your Bias?** This exercise helps students understand that we all can carry biases nurtured by political and social environments that result in emotionally charged views. People can hold fast to ideas that fit their ideology and reject opposing viewpoints. This exercise asks students to recognize and understand the concept of confirmation bias, identify the biases they hold, and question information that reinforces their worldview.
    - (10 minutes) As a class, discuss and come to a consensus on the definitions of the words "bias," "fact," and "opinion." Explain that this exercise allows them the space to explore their views on their topic in order to combat confirmation bias during their research process.
    - (5 minutes) Choose a timely and relevant topic on which most students hold an opinion. Consider something local, like campus parking or alcohol bans on campus. Announce the topic and ask students to write their responses to these questions. Remind them they should ask these questions at the beginning of every research project.
        a. What is my current view on this topic?
        b. Why do I hold this view?
        c. Have I, thus far, read only information resources that support my view?
    - (10 minutes) Divide the class into "pro" and "con." Hand out short articles that support the topic to the "pro" students, and short articles that oppose the topic to the "con" students. Allow this time for reading and reflection, specifically asking students to write down their feelings associated with articles supporting or refuting their views. In the last minute, ask students to quickly name their feelings.
    - (5 minutes) As a class, enumerate three strategies to remain objective while reading alternative viewpoints. This may include such options as researching new concepts or scholars, finding out more context about another person's argument, or taking a viewpoint counter to their own while researching.

3. **What is Their Bias?** This exercise asks students to reflect on how emotionally charged language on social media or news outlets changes or heightens the rhetoric surrounding current events. Additionally, it allows students the opportunity to experience how biased language may change their search results as they complete research online.

- Divide students into discussion groups of no more than four students per group. Each group should have paper or a whiteboard and at least three colors of pen, highlighter, or whiteboard marker. Groups should elect a notetaker and a speaker. Frame the day's events by saying, "Today we are going to investigate how bias and filter bubbles can change the rhetoric and possibly influence the outcome of events in the media."
- (5 minutes) As a class, choose a recent event that was influenced or amplified by social media to frame the day's discussion. It could be a political, criminal, or social event or story that occurred at the national or local level. Take one minute for students to record their views on this event.
- (5 minutes) Have each group define bias and share each definition with the class. Come to a class consensus on the definition of bias.
- (5–10 minutes) In their small groups, students will brainstorm everything they know about the chosen current event, first from the point of view of a supporter of the event, then from the point of view of an opponent of the event. The notetaker should record all ideas in two columns.
- (5 minutes) Ask each group to do two Google searches: one from the point of view of a supporter of the event and one from the point of view of an opponent of the event. The notetaker should record the differences in the search results.
- (10 minutes; 2 minutes per group) Have the students share their knowledge with the larger group and collate the larger themes on a whiteboard.
- (10 minutes) Questions for class discussion: Was it difficult to take a side that is different than your own beliefs? What kinds of emotions came up as you discussed this topic in the small group? Did everyone in your group feel the same way? Were there conflicting perceptions? How did that make you feel?
- (10 minutes) To conclude the class, introduce the concepts of confirmation bias and "filter bubbles." Explain what we currently know about how fake news and social media are used to alter public perception about people, places, and events. Ask students how they find information that challenges their assumptions and considers multiple points of view—or if they don't, how they might go about doing so. Give students a handout or link to a guide containing questions to ask to determine bias.

Engaged Communication

In the workplace, Engaged Communication is an embodied act. In chapter 3, we asked you to become adept at nonverbal communication, practice deep listening, and take part in deliberate two-way communications. Transferring this to the act of research, Engaged Communication can deepen a student's understanding of the material they are researching through structured engagement with other scholars. The ACRL frames that map to this ideal are Scholarship as Conversation and Research as Inquiry, with knowledge practices and dispositions that include the recognition of ongoing scholarly conversations, their own contributions to these conversations, and the power and privilege inherent in disciplinary studies.

Embedded 360 Learning Exercises

1. **Whose Voices Are Here?** This scaffolded annotation exercise will help students organize material so major themes and voices become apparent. After completing this exercise, students will have a better understanding of what scholars are saying about their topic and what is missing from the scholarly conversation. They will have an opportunity to reflect on whose voices are included in the literature, whose are not, and how and why they should include a wide variety of voices in their research projects. To prepare for this exercise, each student should have found and read at least one source, and they should bring this source to class.
   - (5 minutes) Explain to students that understanding the content of their sources and viewpoint of the authors is an essential part of the research process. In addition to taking careful notes containing each source's main ideas as it pertains to their research project, they should be able to articulate what is missing or what has not been addressed in the source. When they understand what is and is not contained in each source, they will know what kinds of articles they need to find going forward.
   - (10 minutes) Hand out the following list of sentence starters on a worksheet. Ask students to complete the first two sentences. The next three sentences can be completed after they have accumulated more source material for their projects.
     - This author tells me that…
     - Because of this author, I now know…
     - This author agrees or disagrees with other authors I've read in that…
     - The author's claims are valid or invalid because…
     - This author has changed or confirmed my viewpoint because…
   - (10 minutes) To scaffold this exercise, ask students to determine whose views or voices are not represented in the source. For example, if a male anthropologist writes about women's lives, how did he get his information? Who is his informant, and are they male or female? If a journalist reports that a city council is taking action in a "blighted

neighborhood," did the journalist interview both city council members and neighborhood residents for their article? Have the students complete the sentence starters on the back of their worksheet.
    o   The author uses the following sources or informants:
    o   Since the author is writing about _____, they could also include the following sources or informants:
- (5–10 minutes) Report back: How does the lack of one or more viewpoints or voices privilege other voices? What is problematic about that?
- (10 minutes) Brainstorm with students how they might go about finding and using sources that contain underrepresented voices. Be specific: if students list "interviews" as their source, ask them who they are going to interview, how they will go about securing that interview for this specific project, and so on.

2. **Can You Hear It?** In this exercise, students partner up to "listen" deeply to an article. Students identify their perceptions of the author's intentions, perspectives, and tone and in so doing learn to modulate their own reactions to source material, reading carefully and critically for the information contained therein.
    - (5 minutes) Ask students to partner with one other student. Allow them time to introduce themselves to one another.
    - (10 minutes) Hand out a short article, preferably one that could be interpreted in many different ways or one that could be considered controversial in the field of study. Ask students to read the article and briefly write down their thoughts about the results or opinions contained in the article.
    - (10 minutes) After each person has written something, share those thoughts with a partner. Ask students to frame their sharing by saying "My perception of this article's results (or conclusions) is…" Make sure both partners have a chance to share their perceptions. Ask students to be actively curious and ask a few clarifying questions to gain a better understanding of their partner's perspective on the article's results or conclusions.
    - (10 minutes) Ask students to change their conversation to assumptions. Each student should finish this sentence: "My assumptions about this article (or author, or research project) are…"
    - (10 minutes) Ask students to consider and question the tone and perspective of the article. Each student should finish this sentence: "The author's tone appears to be _____, especially when they are writing about _____." Ask students to establish whether or not the tone and perspective of the author shows a clear bias in the results or conclusions.

- (Remaining class time) Conclude with a class discussion about why it is important to identify your own perceptions and assumptions along with the author's tone and perspective.

Engaged Communication
Amy Hermodson

We are now living in an age where we are no longer primarily concerned about access but rather the degree to which people succeed or struggle when they use technology to navigate environments, solve problems, and make decisions. In particular, studies on technology usage point to a need for people to develop the ability to determine the trustworthiness of information gathered online, as a significant percentage of US Americans (60 percent) say they find it difficult to know whether the information they find online is trustworthy (Pew, 2016). So how might we use mindfulness practices to help us do this?

When teaching information literacy to students, I incorporate a common mindfulness practice into the lessons to help students develop awareness, reflection, and engagement skills with the information itself and with their classmates. In the first part of this practice, I have each student focus on their own relationship with potential information they might use for an assignment. The individuals are asked to find the very best information they believe meets minimum standards of authority, timeliness, credibility, accuracy, and is free from bias. In the second part of the practice, the students are assigned to small groups of two or three classmates. The classmates are assigned with the task of scrutinizing the sources their group found. This activity is framed as a helping exercise in which we are trying to make sure our classmates have the very best sources for their assignment as possible. If we find any source that doesn't meet the standards previously mentioned (e.g., they can't find who wrote the source, the content appears to be an opinion piece versus fact piece, the source has statistics that can't be verified, etc.) then the group works on finding a replacement source together. I have found that this part of the mindfulness exercise leads to some very engaging, honest, and open conversations among classmates with regard to the trustworthiness of sources. Increased collaborative behaviors such as giving each other tips on how to find trustworthy sources are also a common result of this exercise. The last step of the mindfulness practice asks the student and the peers in their group to imagine a neutral or even oppositional person and how that person would assess the trustworthiness (or potential bias) of the sources. When asked to play "devil's advocate," the students often find parts of their sources that could be even more trustworthy, and they tend to work together to find another source that could be perceived as trustworthy by nearly all audience members.

Through this three-step mindfulness practice, students are given the opportunity to not just learn how to assess source trustworthiness better but also enhance their own ability to become more emotionally aware, practice engaged communication and receive reassurance in that process, and empathetically reflect and take appropriate action in other areas of information literacy.

Author Bio
Dr. Amy Hermodson is a professor of communication studies specializing in interpersonal, conflict/mediation, culture, social media/information literacy, and social support communication. In her personal life, she has been doing mindfulness meditation and yoga practice for over ten years. She has incorporated many of these principles into the courses that she teaches on a regular basis, including the exercise she has submitted here for 360 Framework Ideal in Practice.

Empathetic Reflection and Action

Empathetic Reflection and Action is an ongoing and circular process of awareness of self and others. This ideal teaches students about using empathy, reflection, and agency during the course of their research project. Empathetic reflection asks students to contemplate the impact their research and citation will have on others. Agency ensures students feel empowered and compelled to step forward when you, the instructor, step back. Agency drives students to conceive of themselves as researchers and experts. It encourages students to understand that by using their research skills they can influence conversations in the classroom and beyond. The ACRL frames Authority is Constructed and Contextual, Scholarship as Conversation, and Information Has Value are deeply embedded in this ideal as students engage with their source material and find their place in the scholarly conversation.

Embedded 360 Learning

1. **What Are We Talking About?** In this exercise, students will use the extended metaphor of conversation to create a framework of academic integrity and apply it to an existing body of scholarship using the jigsaw classroom cooperative learning technique. This extended exercise may extend over several class sessions, or students can complete their readings prior to class. The readings are contained in jigsaw packets for groups of five students. The theme of these packets should be a blatant academic integrity violation such as the study published by Andrew Wakefield that falsely concluded that immunizations were causing autism in British children.[4] If it is an advanced course, the jigsaw packet should include the original study, another study that attempted to replicate the findings, the retraction, a news article about the study, and an editorial or reflection piece about the study's effect on public perception. If it is a lower-level course, split one easily skimmed news item into five sections. Each item or section should be numbered, and each student should read one item or section. All packets should contain the same articles.
    - (5 minutes) Introduce the day's practice of ethically entering into a scholarly conversation. Remind students they enter into conversations all the time. For instance, ask students:
        - If you want to meet someone new but don't want to introduce yourself, what do you do? You might ask someone to introduce you, join a club that person is in, or go to a party or other event that person will be at.
        - What do you typically want to know about someone when you first meet them? Their name, career, hobbies, music they listen to, classes they're taking, any mutual friends, and so on.
    - (5 minutes) Conversing with scholarly material is much the same. As a parallel to the question above, ask students: When you are deciding whether or not to use a source, what are some of the things about a source that are important to consider? Their name, affiliations, whether they are discussing information you'll use in your paper, and more.
    - (5 minutes) Explain the importance of citing others' work in your own research projects. You might say, "As students and scholars, there is an

expectation that our work will reflect and interact with that of prior scholars in the field. We are all expected to understand the scholarly conversation we are about to enter and introduce the reader to all of the scholars we have met along the way. Engaging in a scholarly conversation in this fashion lends credibility to your research report. Furthermore, it is the scholar's responsibility to understand academic integrity when entering the conversation. Whether intentional or unintentional, an author's lack of academic integrity produces real-world repercussions. So, what does it mean when I say academic integrity?" As a class, make a list of academic integrity violations. Examples include intentional and unintentional plagiarism, stealing or purchasing research papers, falsifying results of a study, undisclosed payments for research, and ethical violations.

- (5 minutes) Introduce the activity: "Let's get into a discussion about academic integrity and how it might have an impact on our world. To do this, you will get into groups. Each person in the group will read a different article (or a section of one article), and thus they are the expert of that article (or section that article). Then we'll break apart into expert groups to make sure everyone agrees on the top two discussion points in their article (or section). After the section expert groups are finished, we'll come back to our original groups to gain an understanding of the article as a whole, discuss the ethical implications of this research, and how that connects to academic integrity."
- (15 minutes) Hand out the jigsaw packets to each group and have each student read one article or section. To save time, students may complete their reading ahead of time.
- (10 minutes) After students have read and understood their article or section, have them join their expert group and determine the top two main points of their article or section.
- (10 minutes) Have students re-form their original groups and teach the top two main points of their article or section to each other. For best understanding, they should go in order of their numbered article or section.
- (15 minutes) Ask students to critically reflect on and discuss:
    o How was this information originally published and disseminated?
    o Do you think the researchers knew the information was false at the time?
    o Do you get the sense that the researchers were using prior knowledge of their field in an ethical manner?
    o How and why was it ultimately discredited?

- - Is false information still being disseminated using this study as proof? How?
  - Were there repercussions in the original field of study? What were they?
  - What kind of economic repercussions happened as a result of this study?
- (5 minutes) Bring the discussion back to their practice. Ask students, "Even though you may not yet be publishing in medical journals, what are some practices you'll undertake to make sure you're researching in an ethical manner, with integrity?"

2. **What's on the Record?** This exercise uses Wikipedia editing to promote teamwork and agency among students. It is helpful, but not essential, to have additional co-teachers or advanced students who are familiar with Wikipedia's editing software to facilitate this exercise. This exercise is best for students who have basic knowledge of research methods.
   - (10–15 minutes) Facilitate a class discussion about Wikipedia. Consider asking questions about usage, perception, and potential bias of information.
     - How do you use Wikipedia? How does your usage differ in your personal and academic research?
     - What do you think about the amount of "truth" it contains? How much does that matter?
     - Has anyone ever looked up something in Wikipedia and not been able to find it? Why do you think that is? Is there a bias on Wikipedia?
   - (5 minutes) Form teams of four students with at least one facilitator in each group. Have students write down one thing they love, are really good at, obsessed with, and so on. Tell them they will be sharing with their teams and promoting this idea as a potential Wikipedia topic edit idea. Remind students that there is a distinct lack of diverse representation in Wikipedia, and this is their chance to fill in the record.
   - (5–10 minutes) Decide on a topic. Within each team, students announce their idea and make the pitch for this idea as the article to edit. Part of this time could consist of searching Wikipedia to see if the article already exists and has claims that need to be researched and cited.
   - (30 minutes) Check, edit, and cite Wikipedia entries. Using Wikipedia's best practices and the VisualEditor, have each team agree on and complete at least one improvement to a single Wikipedia entry, using research methods learned in previous instruction sessions. Circulate among teams, offering suggestions for reliable and open source material.

- (5–10 minutes) Check in with students. Was this difficult? Were you able to find the "best" sources? How does it feel to fill in the record? Do you think these edits will remain? Why or why not?

Reassurance

Reassurance is an act that must flow from librarian to student in the classroom and during consultations. More than showing students where to click in databases, the most valuable instruction time should be allotted for mentoring students in self-assuring thoughts and acts and advising students to be patient and persistent in the face of frustration and failure. Students should learn how to share their research success with each other and guide one another through the low spots. This ideal maps to Searching as Strategic Exploration, with special emphasis on persistence and guidance throughout their research trajectory.

Embedded 360 Learning

1. **Where Does This Map Take Us?** In this exercise, students will learn how to use brainstorming and mind mapping as a resiliency tool during the topic formation phase of research. Students will learn how to brainstorm as a team and create connections between new ideas as they form research questions together. As class begins, ask students to sit in teams of no more than five students. Give each team an extra-large piece of paper or their own whiteboard with markers. As an alternative to paper, use a class Google Doc or a free online mind mapping tool.
   - (5 minutes) As a class, select a topic that fits the class assignment—for example, mass transit in your local community.
   - (5 minutes) Have each team agree on a population, individual, community, or concept that is affected by or part of the larger topic. Write that word or phrase in the middle of the page and circle it. For example, the five teams in your classroom could be brainstorming about students, Metro Transit drivers, low-income residents, the mayor, and small business owners.
   - (10–15 minutes) Brainstorm things that are important to, or a concern of, the population, individual, or community with regard to the larger class topic. Write each idea, circled, in a bullseye pattern around the central word, connecting each new bubble to the main idea with a line. Your group working on student concerns about mass transit may include ideas like timetables, low cost, direct routes to universities and study spots, easy access to dorms, safety, and room on transit for backpacks or bikes.

- (15–20 minutes) Brainstorm one more "circle" to the bullseye pattern by writing down things that feed into, affect, or are part of the previous group of ideas. Continue writing and connecting each new bubble to an existing idea. For instance, direct routes may need more buses, large enough streets and intersections for additional bus traffic, and safe stops for riders. Students may find that two ideas connect at this level: both timetables and direct routes may need more buses to create change. Have them connect these ideas with a line.
- (10 minutes) Ask students to create at least two research questions from their mind maps by working backward through the bullseye pattern and choosing key ideas. For instance, "How can our city create new mass transit routes without adding to traffic congestion in order to safely serve university students?"
- (5–10 minutes, optional) Encourage students to circulate around the room and find similarities or connections between the maps. Ask them to call out the connections and write each one on the board.
- (5 minutes) Wrap up the session by reiterating the power of brainstorming for topic and research question generation. Remind students that if they mind map their own topic, they can adjust their question as they go, using the ideas generated from this practice. Hand out a blank bullseye mind map for them to fill in on their own.

2. **Could You Use This Source?** This exercise encourages students to take an interest in each other's scholarship and introduces them to the idea of information-sharing during the research process. It works best with small upper-level seminars that have already been introduced to the bibliographic management tool Zotero (www.zotero.org) earlier in the semester or in previous courses.
   - (15 minutes) Have each student present their research ideas to the class. This low-stakes presentation should begin with "I'm working on…" and include the phrase, "I'm looking for sources about…".
   - (15 minutes) Group students together by overall topic. Have each group log in to or create accounts in Zotero and create a new group for themselves.
   - (5 minutes) Explain the concept of information-sharing. Remind them that researching by yourself but having another group of scholars in mind when you're looking for source material and sharing sources that may be helpful with another person is not cheating.
   - (Remaining class time) Proceed with an explanation of database searching if necessary. Have students save their sources to Zotero and upload at least one source to a group member's file.

3. **Will You Be There to Help?** While not an in-class exercise, it is reassuring to students if you offer to set up appointments with them midway through

their research process. Check in with them to find out how their research is progressing, where they might be having difficulties, and what skills taught in the instruction sessions seemed clear then but might be difficult now. If it works in your schedule, offer an option to meet again at a date near the due date of the project for last-minute review.

ENDNOTES

1. Association of College & Research Libraries, *Framework for Information Literacy for Higher Education*, Association of College and Research Libraries, January 11, 2016, http://www.ala.org/acrl/standards/ilframework.
2. Daniel Barbezat and Mirabai Bush, *Contemplative Practices in Higher Education: Powerful Methods to Transform Teaching and Learning* (San Francisco: Jossey-Bass, 2014), 16.
3. Constance A. Mellon, "Attitudes: The Forgotten Dimension in Library Instruction," *Library Journal* 113, no. 14 (September 1, 1988): 137. Mellon's original research can be found in her article, "Library Anxiety: A Grounded Theory and Its Development," *College & Research Libraries*, March 1986, https://doi.org/10.5860/crl_47_02_160.
4. Laura Eggertson, "Lancet Retracts 12-Year-Old Article Linking Autism to MMR Vaccines," *CMAJ : Canadian Medical Association Journal* 182, no. 4 (March 9, 2010): E199–200, https://doi.org/10.1503/cmaj.109-3179.

CHAPTER 8

360 Librarian Practice in Reaching Out and Marketing the Library

Planning outreach and marketing based on 360 Librarian ideals ensures you remain authentic to your institution as you define your purpose and establish a working plan for your library. Outreach and marketing can invite new people into the library, create new partnerships, strengthen existing partnerships, communicate the value of your library, or just delight people who will become your biggest champions. For some libraries, it will help create moments of wonder, whimsy, and play. For others, it will acknowledge that the library is more than just a stereotype of shushing and books. For many, it announces the library as the place for information of all kinds and marks the library as the place to indulge and satisfy all curiosities.

Embedding 360 Librarian ideals in library outreach and marketing allows librarians the space to notice and create connections. Within this mindful space, we have the ability to separate ourselves from our emotional responses and view the image of the library from diverse perspectives. We can investigate how people outside our closest circle are responding to the physical space, the services, and the programming currently in place. In this chapter, we recount some of our own moments of connection created by 360 Librarian practices and explain how those moments forged new relationships, extended the reach of our libraries, or influenced us to takes steps to be more inclusive every day.

360 Outreach and Marketing Planning

Library outreach and marketing planning can take different forms depending on the end goal. A multi-year rebranding effort or a major fundraising drive may be formal committee-driven processes, while smaller outreach partnerships or events may coalesce organically through community networking or library brainstorming sessions. Many outreach moments that are informed by 360 Librarian ideals are as ad hoc as 360 Librarianship itself. Therefore, the following suggested planning steps are not all-inclusive or linear but rather a general guideline for the many possible phases of marketing or outreach planning.

1. Select a planning team (internal team and possibly external partners). If your organization does not employ an outreach or marketing person, gather the people on your team who have outreach and marketing skills. Who is your go-to project manager? Who is good at relationship-building? Who has endless wit and can write your advertising copy? Who has an eye for signage or graphic design? Which person is calm during your busiest programs? Those are the people who should be on your planning teams, regardless of their roles in the organization. Ask for volunteers for each planning team and share the load of outreach and marketing if you can. External partners should align with your goals of each program or partnership and because of this may be invited to join the planning team after the project has been assessed and defined.
2. Assess project and define audience, goals, objectives, and partners. Use this time to refine your project or program. Listen to your students using many different channels: social media, face-to-face conversations, whiteboards, and focus groups. Understand who you want to reach, why you need to reach them, how you plan to reach them, and what success looks like for this specific project or program.
3. Create a timeline, design, and plan. After you have established a date for your program or a due date for your project, work backward to set your timeline. For programs, when do you have to have your advertising turned in to your marketing channels? When do you have to send

invitations? When do you have to book rooms or place your catering order? For projects, when do you want to roll out your deliverables? When is your final report due? Set those due dates and assign specific projects to your team members to ensure work continues between team meetings.
4. Implement. Roll out your project or hold your program. Document and celebrate your success as you do. Remember to collect qualitative and quantitative documentation—for example, the number of attendees as well as their feedback, pictures, or stories—for assessment purposes after your event. During implementation, you may have to make adjustments if you notice things aren't going as planned. Be flexible and mindful of your goals and objectives.
5. Reflect, assess, and communicate results. Within a week of project completion, call a final team meeting to reflect on your results. Could you have done anything better? Do you want to change any part of the process the next time you undertake a similar project or program? How will you "go bigger" next time? After this reflection session, collate the team's ideas along with the documentation from the rollout or event itself and report these results to your organization's leadership team, board, or external partners.

Mindful Practice

Mindful Practice can help librarians understand the needs of their students. The act of creating mental space as part of a personal mindful practice will allow you to notice and assess the needs and desires of your community. Be present and aware as you work, noting possible opportunities for special events, relationship-building, or communication efforts. Remain nonjudgmental with your assessments and notes as you look for causes, effects, and opportunities for authentic personal or institutional interactions. Does this problem have a quick solution that is clearly in your purview to address, or do you have to gain administrative approval?

As a mindful practice focused on assessing how welcoming your library space is to your patrons, consider completing a kindness audit. A kindness audit examines library spaces from the viewpoint of a new visitor for commendable areas and places that could use improvement. Typically, the following questions are used to drive a kindness audit: Is the signage positive? Is the service desk welcoming? Can patrons find their way easily? What obstacles do they encounter? The answers to these questions then drive improvements to the physical space.

A 360 Outreach Moment

The administration of UNO Libraries brought together four recent library hires to undertake a kindness audit after reading about the positive outcomes of kindness audits at other libraries.[1] The audit team members held different roles in the library: a librarian, a front desk supervisor, a reference associate, and a student employee. The team was given *carte blanche* to determine the scope, process, and outcome of the audit. The only provision the team was given was to provide leadership with a report at the end of the project.

Together, the audit team identified eight different areas of the library to investigate: main entrance, service desks, computer areas, third floor, study rooms, classrooms, bathrooms and elevators, and open study areas. For each area, the team developed a walk-through guide with a set of questions to help them notice signage, lighting, obstacles, and furniture. Each member of the audit team completed their audit individually, taking photos and notes of commendable or improvement areas. During several meetings, the team shared photos and notes and came to a consensus regarding six main areas of concern and clear recommendations for improvement. The entire audit, including an executive summary report, was completed in two months. Within two years, the majority of these recommendations, which ranged from fixing a public telephone to painting walls and installing new signage, were implemented.

Emotional Awareness

Librarians who use Emotional Awareness in outreach and marketing consider what others will see and experience in the library and, consequently, ensure all experiences at the library are reassuring and positive. Emotional Awareness in outreach and marketing is the act of critically examining your library's space and understanding the emotional impact art or book displays, images on the library webpage, or signage has on your community. It is an active display of empathy and a willingness to engender changes in the library to ensure dynamic and inclusive displays, programs, and advertising.

A 360 Outreach Moment

Winona, MN sits on a swath of land along the eastern shore of the Mississippi River originally belonging to the Dakota people. The history of the colonization and expulsion of Native Americans from their land has historically been portrayed in art across the Winona State University campus, including in the library. Inside the library, glass display cases on the second floor house reproductions of Frederic Remington's bronze sculptures, many of which depict Native Americans in battle with, or defeated by, colonial soldiers.

The donated artwork stands as a constant grim reminder of the region's brutal colonial past. A student worker in the library, the founder of the Turtle Island Student Organization, a student group formed to spread awareness about the First Nations of Turtle Island and to work with the community for a more equitable environment, shared how demoralizing it felt to sit at the circulation desk knowing that the genocide of Native Americans was being depicted in the display cases one floor above her.

University administration listened to the concerns of the members of the Turtle Island Student Organization and, with the help of the university's staff and faculty Arts Collection Committee, devised a plan for art depicting Native Americans across campus to be contextualized with interpretive labels. In the library, while the Arts Collection Committee negotiated the task of moving the donated Remington reproductions elsewhere on campus or contextualizing them with new labels, a new temporary exhibition titled *Water Protectors* was installed. In stark contrast to the Remington reproductions, the *Water Protectors* photograph series depicts images of the Dakota people protesting the Dakota Access Pipeline. The visceral response invoked by the strength of the Dakota people depicted in the photographs made an indelible impression on viewers during the run of the exhibition. The exhibition was a powerful and moving tribute to Native Americans and to the students who worked hard to make a change.

Emotional Awareness
Molly Hart

Columbia College Chicago is a nonprofit college offering a distinctive undergraduate and graduate curriculum that blends creative and media arts, liberal arts, and business, located in downtown Chicago. As a library on an urban campus, we often struggle to compete with myriad resources provided by the city. As the Student Engagement Coordinator, I wanted to better understand how the library impacted our students and helped gather a small group of current students for an informal meeting.

The goal of this meeting was to gain a sense of how our students perceive the library. What services were they aware of? What services were they unaware of? What kinds of workshops and social activities would they like the library to host? After introductions (and the traditional offering of pizza and soda) I started by asking a few basic questions. "What kind of workshops should the library host?" Blank stares. I rephrase the question, "What kinds of skills would you like to learn?" Crickets. At this point, I could feel the tumbleweeds blow through the small room. I looked down at my list of questions. All of them revolved around big, scary ideas like the future. I realized that I was asking a lot; not only was I asking them to reveal the personal strengths and weaknesses, but I was asking them how those strengths and weaknesses could be capitalized on for future programming. The obvious suddenly dawned on me: figuring out how students could benefit from the library was my job, not theirs! I needed to back up, to ground the conversation in something personal.

"What are you afraid of?" Suddenly, their eyes lit up. They started stumbling over each other to answer, "I have no idea how to manage my time. I'm afraid I won't make it to graduation." Ah, a workshop on time-management. "I have no idea how to say no and I'm... exhausted." A workshop on personal and professional boundaries, perhaps. When I asked for workshop ideas, they didn't know what I was talking about, but when I asked them about their hopes and fears, the workshop ideas flowed. By simply using more emotional language—language our students were more familiar with—I learned about their strengths as well as their vulnerabilities.

For the most part, people are ready and willing to tell you how they feel. It's up to you to understand how those feelings can and should affect your library. I encourage anyone reading this to reduce their questions to their emotional core. By asking straightforward questions, we encourage honesty and often find our students brimming with ideas.

Author Bio

Molly Hart is currently the manager of operations in the Vice President of Student Affairs office at Columbia College Chicago. She served as the student engagement coordinator at Columbia College Chicago Library from 2014-2018. She holds a BA in women's studies from Mills College.

Engaged Communication

Weaving Engaged Communication through the planning stages of your marketing project or outreach event allows you to connect with other people in your community. To do this, remain fully engaged with your own and others' verbal and nonverbal cues as you hold focus groups or brainstorm in committee to determine the services your library should offer to the community. Engage in frank conversations with others to understand how they feel when they enter the building, participate in an outreach activity, or interact with staff. Listen deeply, limit distractions, and show your partners you are committed to their ideas by empowering them to implement their suggestions. Sustain this embodied and purposeful connection into the implementation phase as you roll out your marketing project or hold your event. Consider incorporating Engaged Communication into library services by offering special events that encourage widely inclusive experiences, deep listening, or thoughtful discussion. Some examples include bilingual storytimes, drag queen storytimes, or the Human Library.

A 360 Outreach Moment

The international Human Library movement began in 2000 at the Roskilde Festival in Denmark. The organizers wanted to challenge stereotypes and prejudices by encouraging people with different backgrounds to have real dialogues in a safe and affirming space. In Human Library terms, human "books" are checked out by "readers" who converse with people they might not otherwise meet in the course of their everyday lives. During the first Human Library in Denmark, fifty people with diverse life experiences were available over the course of the entire festival. A total of 1,000 readers checked out human books eight hours a day for four days straight. Since then, hundreds of Human Libraries have taken place all over the world.

UNO Libraries has convened a Human Library every year since 2015. The local event began at the suggestion of one library staff member who wanted to celebrate National Library Week by replicating the Danish event on campus. The first year, two organizers asked ten people to volunteer to be human books for twenty-three readers. The event has grown exponentially since then. For the most recent Human Library, dozens of community members applied to be one of fifteen books. Enhanced social media marketing and invitations to students in campus learning communities resulted in more than seventy-five readers during the three-hour event, and dozens more were turned away after the event was fully booked. Positive responses from both books and readers, along with significant media coverage of this unique event, encourages organizers and library administration to continue hosting the Human Library each year.

Empathetic Reflection and Action

Empathetic Reflection and Action is a continual deep practice in concert with other ideals. It is a patron-centered activity with a service orientation that percolates through all steps of a marketing or outreach event plan. Develop empathy for your patrons while you assess their needs and define your project goals. Take care not to discount their struggles or fears. Remember that, for example, using a self-check scanner may be easy or fun for you, but it isn't for everyone. Question each assumption you hold about your patrons, their needs, their desires, and your services as you design and plan your marketing or event. Do your services and resources actually meet their needs and desires? Is the event you are planning going to supplement or highlight your services and resources, or in some other way serve your population—if even to delight and inspire them? Examine your power structure and examine when, why, and how you make the marketing and outreach decisions you do. Are you part of a power structure, administratively or socially, that hews toward tradition rather than reality? Do you make marketing choices to appear edgy without any substance to bolster your claims? Are you assuming a paternalistic stance? Finally, use occasions like special events or pop-up marketing pushes to decenter yourself, shift agency, and invite others into the process and the outcome.

A 360 Outreach Moment

Conversations with the Turtle Island Student Organization president revealed that the Frederic Remington sculptures at Winona State's Library was one example of systemic microaggressions some students experienced while working at the circulation desk. Some of the white cis faculty found themselves humbled when one university administrator posed questions like, "How might students, faculty and staff of different races, ethnicities, abilities, faiths, genders, and sexualities feel as they enter the library? How do they see themselves represented in the book displays, the artwork, the journals and books in the collection? Is it in a positive or a negative manner? Do they see themselves represented at all?" Some librarians went further to ask themselves if any of the materials in the library promote dangerous stereotypes, medical inaccuracies, or offensive, inaccurate histories. They also questioned what they could do to reach out to students and employees to create an inclusive environment. Conversations among library faculty and staff to answer these questions were difficult as they discussed how, when, and why library administration should change their policies or procedures in response to this feedback.

The link between an inclusive and civil workplace and inclusive outreach and marketing is strong. Employees who feel empowered to point out areas of inequity can offer objective insight into whether or not marketing and outreach plans are inclusive and welcoming. This, in turn, creates a culture where people feel accepted and safe in the library. At Winona State's library, employees were invited to take advantage of civility professional development opportunities to learn how to recognize, understand the impact of, and address microaggressions in the workplace. Student employees received training in workplace civility, microaggressions, and cultural sensitivity. Supervisors reaffirmed their open door policy for student workers to voice concerns in the workplace with a guarantee of no repercussions. Librarians made a conscious effort to create inclusive book displays, and news spread that the library was actively seeking partnerships with faculty and groups on campus to host culturally diverse displays and events in the library.

Reassurance

The act of reassurance replaces doubt or insecurity your staff, partners, or patrons may have with feelings of faith and confidence. Bolstering confidence during outreach and marketing can be enacted during the initial implementation as you roll out special events or marketing materials about services and resources or during the wrap-up phase. Reassurance during the wrap-up phase can include communicating to administration and community partners how your goals have been met in light of the mission and vision of your organization. If the project was unsuccessful, reassurance also includes bolstering the confidence of the planning team as you plan improvements for similar events in the future.

A 360 Outreach Moment

Outreach to college students often reaches its peak during finals week, when many libraries offer reassurance to students to help them through the stress of their final projects and exams. Food giveaways, coloring stations, or offbeat events like a midnight primal scream or silent dance party are classic library de-stress offerings. At the University of Nebraska Omaha, departments from all over campus collaborate on De-Stress Fest, a week of events designed to help students take a break, recharge, and de-stress during prep and finals week. One of the most successful events for the library to date was one designed to comfort students in the cutest way possible—with baby goats. After an event with therapy dogs was found to be popular but difficult to organize because of a lack of community partners, library staff started a running joke that farm animals were next. One semester, the administration agreed and the hunt was on for cute farm animals anywhere in the metro area. Luckily, Omaha remains rural on the margins and goats were rented from a local rescue farm for a nominal fee, and more than 450 students made their way outside the library to hold a baby goat.

Not all De-Stress Fest events have been as successful as baby goats. Many crafting events have had only a few attendees. A gaming event with the dean of the library had one student sit in the room only long enough to be polite. Even some events with food have resulted in library staff delivering popsicles, donuts, or cake to students waiting for shuttle buses outside the library. After these unsuccessful events, self-reassurance has been vital. There are many variables at play that determine the success of an event, including day, time, marketing, title, and even the weather for the event. It is often difficult to determine if low attendance was because the event was a poor fit for the audience or if it was simply an off day. At UNO Libraries, we know that while successful events promote a sense of community for library staff and students and elevate the status of the library for university administration, we often learn more from less successful events. Critical reflection on what could have been done differently, honest feedback through engaged communication with attendees or student workers, and reassurance that there is no need for fear of failure offer priceless lessons. To reassure the planning team even after events with low attendance, we look to our goals and objectives. We know that sometimes we have to consider events a success even if one person attended and now sees the library in a positive light because of their experiences that day.

ENDNOTES

1. Joe Hardenbrook, "Examining Library Spaces Through a Kindness Audit," *Mr. Library Dude* (blog), October 17, 2013, https://mrlibrarydude.wordpress.com/2013/10/17/examining-library-spaces-through-a-kindness-audit/; Joe Hardenbrook and Jessica Olin, "Killing it With Kindness, Incorporating Sustainable Assessment Through Kindness Audits" (presented at the Association of College and Research Libraries virtual conference, May 10, 2015).

CHAPTER 9

360 Librarian Practice in Working with Technology

What does it take to have a moment away from technology in our working lives? For us, it would be difficult to go through a workday without technology. We use email to communicate with coworkers, scanners, and library management systems to process interlibrary loans and check out and return books, chat reference services and online databases to provide service to our patrons, and so much more. On a personal level, technology has infiltrated every aspect of our lives. We are tethered to our laptops and our phones. We wrote this book using Google Docs with several states and, later, continents between us. We use apps to help navigate or arrange our transportation, track fitness, get real-time weather updates, share stories with each other, text our families every day, and read books in every free moment. We both spend far too long each day on social media or streaming services, despite what we know about the feedback loop of apps and social media contributing to our technology addictions. For us, it feels normal to be constantly connected, even as we know that very connection amplifies our anxiety and depression.

For both of us, it takes a conscious effort to walk away from our tech. However, when we do walk away from technology even for a moment, things get better. We breathe easier and notice more. We tend to do more planning and less reacting. For us, less technology means more presence. In this chapter, we examine professional and personal uses of technology through the lens of 360 librarianship. For each 360 ideal, we offer "stop and think" moments to help 360 Librarians break the feedback loop and engage with technology carefully, on purpose and with intention.

Mindful Practice

The difficulty with remaining in the moment while using technology is that phones, computers, or TVs can easily pull you out of a mindful state of connectedness with the world around you. Instead, you become connected to the rush of being that librarian who is always available online and the constancy of being able to check your schedule over and over. While it is impractical to suggest giving up email entirely or just unplugging from devices for long periods of time, you can train your brain to ignore the pull of *mindless* technology. You can integrate technology into your work life in a mindful way, with compassion toward yourself and your role in your organization.

360 Stop and Think Moments

1. Forget your phone. Attend meetings without electronic devices to avoid the distraction. If you must travel with your devices, leave them in your bag instead of on the table. This will allow you to focus your attention on the participants and the discussion and signal to the others in the room that you are focused on them and are interested in their ideas. If you take notes, do so with pen and paper.
2. Turn off your notifications. Pings, popup alerts, and vibrations disrupt your attention. At that moment, you could have been speaking with someone, drafting a budget, designing a course, researching a reference question, or whatever it is you *actually do* during the day, but with those notification sounds your mind is taken out of the flow of doing and placed into the what-if of always-on connection. You are no longer single-pointedly attentive to what is before you. Your mind, in some small way, is beginning to wonder what awaits you on your notification screen. Turn off notifications and check your phone between projects or at lunch.
3. Begin longer projects or email sessions with mindful centering. Find a state of connectedness to your tasks by taking a few seconds to center yourself every time you shift your attention to something new. Stretch your arms, touch your toes, perform five seconds of mindful breathing, or walk around the building or outside for a few minutes. This will reset and calm your mind as you settle down to work.

Emotional Awareness

The human connection to technology is inherently emotional, but everyone approaches technology with a different attitude. As we mentioned above, we both have a somewhat fraught relationship with technology. We know others who have a more balanced attitude toward technology use in their personal and private lives. They tend to have a "take it or leave it" attitude toward technology but understand the importance of software and hardware at work. Others have noticed how technology has made them feel in the past and decided that social media or other technology is not for them. Working with technology using 360 ideals accepts all these mind states and more. Emotional Awareness as a practice simply asks that you notice, assess, and react in the most positive way possible to the emotional states surrounding your technology use.

360 Stop and Think Moments

1. Set your email baseline. For many of us, email uses the largest block of time in the day. To set the baseline of your emotional engagement with email and your mind's reaction to email, use the technique developed by David M. Levy in *Mindful Tech*. Check your email, and as you are doing so notice your physical and emotional reactions to the act of opening, reading, and responding to email. Write down these reactions, including all thoughts and feelings. As you do this a few times over the course of the next day or week, come to a conclusion about your habitual thoughts and emotional reactions to email. Then, formulate a plan to help yourself adjust these thoughts and reactions toward a more calm and helpful frame of mind. Discuss this plan with others.[1]
2. Name and assess the emotions you feel when using *all* technology. Extending David Levy's exercises, take a few minutes throughout your day to record your emotions and reactions to technology in a technology diary. Keep a journal next to you for a week to quickly write down your current work task (group project, updating your workplace's social media, writing email, making appointments, cataloging), the type of technology being used (email, social media, PowerPoint, work-related software), and your emotional state before, during, and after the use of technology. Start a process of change by noticing when you feel most calm and positive using technology, and star those moments in your technology diary.
3. Forget your phone (again). Give yourself permission to step away from your phone or email for a period of time. Check and respond to email or voicemail messages at specific times during the day, even if it is for just

one day during the week. Let this be your time to accomplish goals that need time for extended contemplation.

Engaged Communication

For 360 Librarians, face-to-face communication creates an atmosphere for authentic connection that is difficult to replicate online. While you can "listen" actively through careful reading and interpretation of online communication, the physical cues of nonverbal communication are nonexistent online. Deliberate two-way communication becomes halting when mediated via email, texting, or apps. When engaging in online communication, it is important to do so with great attention to detail and careful thought about your reply.

360 Stop and Think Moments

1. Think twice before emailing about hot issues. Before you react to an emotionally charged email in your inbox, take a moment to process and reflect on the situation rather than firing off a response immediately. Read the sender's original email fully. Consider the context in which they are writing and the emotional weight of their words. Allow for miscommunications of tone. Try reframing what seems like an attack into a more collegial challenge. After you read their email, find the best way to craft your message so that it creates positive connections and adds value. Don't allow this heated moment to later cause regret and remorse for yourself or someone else.
2. Try a face-to-face exchange instead of an email. Your engagement with technology might be impacting the emotions of your colleagues through the tone of your email or text messages. Read your email replies several times for content, then for tone before you send a reply. Or get out of your office and reply to an email with a face-to-face chat. This is a good option if you think your written tone might be misconstrued, if what you have to say will take longer to type than to say, and if you don't need to keep a written reminder of your decisions or actions.
3. Engage with a wide community online. Joining online communities offers you the opportunity to connect with people you would not ordinarily be able to meet in person. You can share information and accomplish tasks together regardless of physical location. To find your online community, cast a wide net. Join traditional listservs or build your own personal email circles. There are Facebook groups for almost every kind of library and every role in libraries. Join them or create your own. Find other librarians wherever you hang out online. Don't be afraid to engage in meaningful conversation with others, no matter how large or small the community might be.

Empathetic Reflection and Action

Using empathy and reflection, 360 Librarians can learn about the situational context of technology use and react considerately and appropriately to current digital practices in their personal and professional lives. You can decide what works for you, what hinders your daily productivity, and how you want to use technology to create moments of agency for yourself and others.

360 Stop and Think Moments

1. Analyze your reactions to technology at work. Look through the diary of emotions attached to your technology use. When you analyze your emotional state while using technology over an entire day or week, which emotions are are most prominent? Are you comfortable with the range of emotions you are experiencing? What areas would you like to change? Once you understand how technology makes you feel, take action. Try to do more with the projects and technology that create positive feelings. Try to turn negative feelings to more positive ones by developing offline connections. If you're feeling disconnected because you have to sit in front of your computer for much of the workday, for example, meet a colleague for a working lunch instead.
2. Reflect on when you do (and don't) use technology. Be honest with yourself about your habits. Do you use technology to avoid a colleague? Do you write emails to avoid hard conversations? Does laptop use in departmental meetings cause disconnection, or encourage collaboration? If you feel disconnected from your colleagues, try to find ways to use technology less and talk directly to each other more. Do you use PowerPoint presentations during teaching sessions? Do you need to? Try to connect with students by using technology, such as database demonstrations, only when absolutely essential. As part of your 360 Librarian practice, use less technology as you become more confident in your ability to communicate directly with those around you.
3. Ensure your technology use fits with your outcomes. For teaching librarians, new technology is sometimes used in lieu of an outcome, rather than as a means to accomplish or assess an outcome. Use some forms of technology such as clickers or online polling software to interact with more people in a large classroom. Don't be afraid to use low-tech teaching strategies such as discussion and minute papers to create engaging and authentic learning moments in your classroom.

Reassurance

Reassurance is the act of bolstering one's own and others' confidence through a variety of means. If a form of technology has negative connotations for you, you might need reassurance that you can disconnect from that technology without repercussions. You can also use technology for positive outcomes as you develop relationships and create shared moments that may not otherwise occur.

360 Stop and Think Moments

1. Forget your phone (yet again). This time, leave your phone at home for an entire workday. For many of us, this is cause for extreme anxiety, but it is a useful lesson in reassurance that you can get through a whole workday without it. Work through or forget the anxiety as you do your daily tasks. Remind yourself that you are still connected to your loved ones and your colleagues in different ways. Find ways to fill the time you would normally spend on your phone and notice what you accomplish when you would otherwise check out for a few minutes. Notice what you do better when you have your phone and the workarounds you had to develop without it.
2. Type carefully and thoughtfully. When you write emails to your colleagues and chat with students online, be thoughtful about how formal you sound online. Periods at the end of every sentence can come across as flat or angry. Use exclamation points every so often to express excitement and positivity but not so often as to come across as silly, especially in email. Use emojis with students in chat but not in emails. Students tend to view email as a necessary communication device that is used at work, so the formality level of chat can be much lower than it is in email. Smiley faces to reassure students in chat messages are very welcome, so use them at will. Just make sure you know the connotation and denotation of every emoji before you use it, or you might end up embarrassing yourself on social media or in chat.
3. Use shared documents to work collaboratively. Shared meeting minutes and documents on wikis and organization-wide servers allows people from the entire organization to work toward goals and monitor the progress of large projects together. In these shared and transparent spaces, everyone can freely share feedback and bolster one another with public rewards and kudos.

Reassurance
Wendy Doucette

I oversee a suite of graduate-level research support workshops open to graduate students and faculty. Divided into "Beginner" and "Advanced," "Beginner" skills (understanding the research process, searching, project management, and data) are needed immediately upon beginning a graduate program. "Advanced" covers deeper skills required for students in their second year and beyond. While we incorporate the 360 Framework ideals of mindfulness and empathy into the entire series, I want to highlight the example of working with technology in teaching "Infographics for Academics" in a way that is grounded, reflective, and collaborative.

In "Academic Publications and Presentations," the first workshop of the "Advanced" series, I explain the various ways research is traditionally presented: paper, poster, presentation. I include "survival skills" strategies for live presentations and demonstrate qigong exercises for remaining centered and breathing calmly under stress. "Infographics for Academics" builds upon the academic need to present and explores means of communicating visually to a potentially worldwide audience.

While students pursue graduate degrees for a variety of reasons, however altruistic their motivation, the ultimate goal after the attainment of the degree is employment. Unlike publications and presentations—something students are reluctant to do but know they must—using infographics is optional. As a desirable extra in high demand in any workplace, understanding infographics is perceived to be a real-world asset. Unlike so much of the traditional academic skillset, removing the constraint of "required for graduation" removes the pressure of having (and perhaps failing) to learn.

With no background or generally even exposure to the topic, the openness of a new concept in a stress-free environment allows students the freedom of "beginner's mind." Although I cover a variety of software for making infographics, I don't teach it step-by-step. Software companies provide comprehensive tutorials, and the amount of time required would be prohibitive. The technology is subservient to the greater concept of becoming creators capable of transmitting data into meaningful stories. My function is to ground the material as a means to an end in the larger context of visual communication.

"Infographics for Academics" is about learning to see with a designer's eye. Intentionally separating the frustrations of doing from conceptual understanding provides reassurance and bolsters confidence that even if students are not able to perform the task yet, they can grasp the underlying purpose.

As a group, we begin by analyzing what is and what is not an infographic. As active participants, we examine form and message. Students make these determinations themselves, evaluating and offering critiques in real time. While consensus is not necessary, discussion is, as is maintaining the emotional awareness and engaged communication to respect each others' opinions and suggestions. Viewing data expressed with color, line, and structure is a revelation to students. This experience of establishing one's self as appreciator and critic prior to imagining oneself in a design role is a logical, yet rare extension of academic output. Creating a persuasive message in a new environment takes on a transformative aspect when students realize their own potential for agency.

Author Bio

Dr. Wendy Doucette is an assistant professor and the graduate research and instruction librarian at East Tennessee State University. She is the lead instructor and developer of the Sherrod Library Graduate-Level Academic Workshop series and an embedded librarian for the Graduate School's Thesis and Dissertation Boot Camp. She holds an MS in library and information science from Florida State University and a PhD from Stanford University. Her research interests center on 360-degree literacy, visual literacy, real-world skills, and supporting international students. She has written on emotion, empathy, and student motivation.

ENDNOTES

1. David M. Levy, *Mindful Tech: How to Bring Balance to Our Digital Lives* (Yale University Press, 2016), 49.

CHAPTER 10

360 Librarian Practice in Leadership

In this chapter, we provide examples a new administrator can use to integrate 360 Librarian ideals in a traditional but transforming academic library. We explain how to use each ideal to lead a department's culture change from a reactionary mode to a proactive one and in the process turn a culture of entrenchment into a culture of experimentation. We show how you can pair compassion and equanimity with confidence and communication to bring a team together during a critical time of change.

In this, we assume several conditions. First, in your role, you have the time and authority to commit to changing your organization's culture. Second, that you have champions in your department or organization who will adapt to and embrace new ways of thinking and doing, and in doing so lead the rest of the department to embrace change as well. Third, that you are personally committed to a mindful and proactive leadership role. You can still lead culture change if these three conditions are not met, but it may be more difficult to do so.

Critical reflection is essential for continual improvement and lasting change in all organizations, but engaging in critical reflection as an organization may be easier in some workplaces than others. Stephen Brookfield writes of three main cultural barriers that must be recognized and overcome by administrators in order for critical reflection to become a cultural norm in workplaces. In a culture of *silence*, employees are acutely aware that workplace conditions, knowingly or not, impede on the opportunity for colleagues to discuss the daily dilemmas, demands, struggles, and successes. Asking for help may be viewed as an admission of substandard performance. In a culture of *individualism*, the organizational structure and workplace culture reward individual effort over collaboration. Collaborative ventures are not acknowledged, funded, and rewarded. Working with colleagues may be perceived as threatening to leadership and is discouraged. In a culture of *secrecy*, an atmosphere of trust isn't present. Weaknesses and failures must be concealed as these are viewed as justification for punishment rather than opportunities for improvement.[1] In this example, we will suggest several ways to overcome silence, individualism, and secrecy in your organization using the 360 Librarian ideals of Engaged Communication, Empathetic Reflection and Action, and Reassurance.

While we use the framework of a new administrator throughout this chapter, we understand leaders from many different areas of the organization are essential for the cultural shifts that bring about change. We hope all leaders, with or without titles, will see themselves in this chapter. Administrative librarians make dozens of small decisions each day to ensure the smooth functioning and future success of the library. Those who lead without titles offer institutional knowledge, revolutionary ideas, morale improvement, and more. All leaders in the library can appreciate the delicate balance of managing their own and others' reactions to the stress and uncertainty of transformational changes.

Mindful Practice

A dedicated mindfulness practice can be a portal into empathetic, relationship-based leadership. Mindfulness helps leaders develop a heightened sense of self-awareness, which can lead to the voluntary improvement of several key components of emotional intelligence like empathy, conflict management, and interpersonal communication.[2] To help develop the personal focus and equanimity needed to change a department's culture, begin with your own daily practice. Several minutes of a mindful practice each morning after you awaken, as described in chapter one, allows your mind to rest for a moment free from worries and complaints. It helps you practice nonjudgmental awareness, which is a healthy habit to develop if your workplace contains colleagues who engage in negative behavior such as bullying or passive-aggressive commentary. Mindful Practice helps you manage your emotions carefully in positive environments and helps develop equanimity, a quality of mind that ensures you will remain steadfast and composed regardless of external forces.

360 Leadership Practice

As you enter the workplace each day, take time at the entrance for yourself, especially if you are expected to be "on" as soon as you arrive. At this moment before you enter the building, set your expectations of positive or negative interactions aside and take three mindful breaths. With these breaths, set your intention for the day, a task previously described in chapter one. These intentions should not be items on your to-do list, but they may intersect with your daily calendar. For instance, if you have a challenging meeting with a supervisor, colleague, or student, your intention may be to listen more and speak less. If you are working on a new policy for your department, your intention may be to see all sides of a situation. If your day is filled with marketing or design for the library, your intention may be to open your creative brain to its utmost. In this particular example, you may spend the first several weeks in your new position setting the intention every day to be open to others' ideas and attitudes.

Once you have set your intentions for the day, turn to your daily tasks. In this example, where you are looking to change the very culture of your library, open your mind to recognize and acknowledge the stickiest situations under your purview—especially those situations or problems that are the linchpins for your desired culture change. Ask yourself: What one thing, if changed, would start this organization moving in what I perceive to be a more positive direction? Choose one of the most pressing situations for which you are responsible and research solutions. This could be accomplished in several ways but completing a quick literature review to find out how other libraries solved similar problems is one common technique. A literature review will help you recognize common situations as they happen and will allow you to adapt and react with calm awareness. Look for case studies in library science and business management literature. Become comfortable with the jargon and look for creative options to address those situations that have calcified or stunted your workplace. Consider speaking with others in the same situation, if you can. Once you have collected best practices from other workplaces, compare it to your own situation. Do you see parallels? Exceptions that are unique to your situation? What questions can you ask to move toward a solution? Do you need to partner with someone to achieve a positive outcome, or can you make a decision and move forward on your own?

Stay with this one sticky situation for the day, and, with calm awareness, let that be foremost in your mind. When you notice unhelpful negative thoughts or anxiety surrounding this sticky situation entering your thoughts, remind yourself that you know others that have surmounted similar difficulties and with time and effort you can as well. If you have more than one problematic area, place your mind on them one at a time with your full concentration. If you can, delegate less-pressing problems to others in the organization. This creates a sense of teamwork and camaraderie and allows you to continue your single-pointed concentration on the most impactful areas.

Emotional Awareness

As a leader and change agent in the library, awareness and management of your own and your team's emotions is a difficult but necessary first step in creating a new management structure and culture change. You may hear stories of extreme dissatisfaction with previous administrative policies or gossip that whispers of a lack of faith in your leadership. You may step into meeting rooms filled with colleagues who project negativity in their body language or word choices. Every time this happens, it can be difficult to open your heart and create meaningful relationships with those colleagues.

360 Leadership Practice

As we discussed in chapter 2, noticing, assessing, and reacting to emotions is paramount for success in the workplace. As you meet with others at all levels of your organization to find out more information about your stickiest situation, notice the emotions you experience while listening to your colleagues. Remind yourself that, as an administrator, your emotional comfort will sometimes be challenged and you are not attached to the emotions that arise in yourself. Put aside your ego and listen carefully to others. Notice their words, body language, and conversational rapport with you and others in your organization.

After each meeting, stop to reflect and assess. What information did you glean about the situation that is factual? Using your knowledge and practice of engaged communication, reflect on the emotions you can infer from the body language and rapport in the room? What emotions were present in their speech? Did their words and body language match? Remember that you are coming into a situation that has had weeks, months, or years to develop. Your team needs time to reframe and rewrite the negative script they have established for their positions and the organization. Regard negative emotions with compassion and give other people—especially those who are not in administration—space and support to present their perceptions of the stickiest situation without judgment or backlash.

Engaged Communication

Leaders who are engaged communicators are active, curious, and deliberate in their listening and speaking. While others are speaking, engaged communicators listen to others instead of thinking of their next comment. They ask questions instead of thinking of or telling stories. They speak to others with an intention of equality and appreciation. This sort of deliberate communication with colleagues supports productive interpersonal interactions and creates a culture of respect and inclusiveness. While untangling your stickiest situation in a time of administrative change, Engaged Communication began with Emotional Awareness as you noticed and reflected on nonverbal communication that expressed negative emotions in first-round inquiry meetings. This noticing and reflection should continue throughout the administrative changes and expand to include an awareness of body language in everyday interactions in the hallways, service desks, and break rooms.

360 Leadership Practice

During the deep listening phase of Engaged Communication for leaders, take the opportunity to do a formal or informal SWOT (Strengths, Weaknesses, Opportunities, Threats) analysis with a team that includes your forward-thinking champions as well as employees who have concerns about your stickiest situation. The SWOT analysis operates as a way for leaders to pull together all the information that is influencing the decision-making process and can be used to help leaders analyze how and when to implement change. First, brainstorm the internal factors, which are the strengths and weaknesses, in relation to the sticky situation you would like to solve or overcome. An honest assessment of strengths and weaknesses allows leaders to take inventory of the resources available as well as the talents and abilities of the team members, which leads to better decision-making. After examining the internal factors, consider the outside forces, or opportunities and threats. Exploring opportunities creates a mindset that encourages a culture of innovation while understanding weaknesses keeps leaders on guard and helps eliminate possible threats that can sabotage culture change.

Empathetic Reflection and Action

A personal practice of empathetic reflection combined with a mindfully cultivated culture of reflection in the workplace leads to an egalitarian workforce that is more likely to complete tasks with cooperation and a sense of camaraderie. Reflecting on your own leadership style allows you to recognize longstanding leadership practices or beliefs that have become invisibly ingrained in your work life. Examining and understanding the motives behind some of your long-held beliefs, like appropriate attire, work ethic, or even what "good enough" looks like, can lead to more empathetic interactions between you and your team. Empathetic interactions between managers and employees have been shown to lead to healthier, more engaged, and successful employees and cultivates a culture of understanding, well-being, and greater happiness.[3]

Thoughtfully operationalized Empathetic Reflection and Action can lead to positive synergy in the library, but employees *must* feel empowered to bring forth the creative ideas generated by the practice of this 360 Librarian ideal in order to generate a lasting culture change. To do that, library administration and change leaders in the library should actively dismantle cultural barriers that stifle empathy, reflection, and action as they model and support inspirational reflective behavior for all employees. Silence, individualism, and secrecy—Brookfield's three barriers to critical reflection—come about via administrative structures that are "too much" in any direction: draconian, impotent, politicized, or consensus-seeking. Colleagues, whether well-meaning or vindictive, can derail new ideas through fear of change or failure, obstructionism, or an unwillingness to work outside siloed job descriptions. Moments of action can be lost because of the encultured feeling that empathy and social justice are secondary to a narrow and unchangeable mission.

Cultural barriers and negativity embedded in the library's institutional memory can be overcome with a leadership team or a dedicated group of employees who are willing to name and describe the elephant in the room. Whether it is as overt as verbal hostility or bullying or as covert as occasional disdain or rudeness, library leaders must reject negative attitudes in the workplace and create a safe environment for empathy and reflection. Empathetic Reflection and Action, when practiced to its fullest extent, is a continual learning process that begins with identifying the root of uncomfortable or ambiguous situations and working together to bring about a positive resolution. As a team, the entire library can provide distinct rewards and pathways to success to normalize a motivational and creative culture, instead of an indifferent or hostile one. In any organization, these situations and their resolutions are deeply connected to the culture and take some time to resolve.

360 Leadership Practice

To begin the process, reflect on your perception of the assumptions, behaviors, and skills that drive your organization's culture. Does silence, individualism, secrecy, or negativity predominate in any department? What do your champions do to solve problems and stay engaged despite dealing with your stickiest situation?

Once you have reflected on questions like these, address your stickiest situation by examining the Engaged Communication SWOT analysis. Your organization's strengths are a direct reflection of your colleagues' unique qualities. Match their skills with action items. Who has a gift for building relationships, who are the cheerleaders, who has the ability to persuade others, and who has the ability to see the big picture versus the fine nuances of the sticky situation? An honest assessment of your organization's weaknesses will provide a snapshot of areas that need improvement. Normalize continuous professional development in your organization in order to help employees turn what could be perceived as weaknesses into opportunities for organizational and personal growth. Channel the positive energy created by brainstorming your organization's opportunities and create goals and action items that align with your organization's mission. Avoid setbacks by examining threats. If one of those threats includes complacent or recalcitrant staff, consider how you might work together to create a shared vision for change.

After completing the SWOT analysis, work collaboratively with your team of influencers to envision the situation through a new lens. Create and document policies for the organization together. Publish any public-facing policies on an easily accessible area of your website and place internal documents on an organizational wiki or in a shared physical or online storage space.

Empathetic Reflection and Action

Carol Daul-Elhindi

As the access services librarian, I am occasionally tasked with handling complaints that have escalated. One afternoon, the front desk manager approached me with a phone message from a former student who had been billed for nineteen unreturned items. The fines and fees associated with these items totaled more than $1,000. When the student failed to act, the bill was sent to collections. Subsequently, the state garnished the patron's income. This, of course, caught the patron's attention and she was turning to the library for help.

I was informed that this patron suffered from what others assumed was delusional paranoia, that she would be difficult to work with, and that I should have a second person in the room when I talked with her to corroborate what was discussed. The message she left noted that she was sure she had returned the books and she had never received notification informing her that the books were overdue. She couldn't understand how this had happened.

I reflected on this information before returning her call. I wondered, how often did people dismiss her when conversations became uncomfortable? How did her confused mental state affect her mood and her daily interactions? Was she experiencing financial difficulty now that her checks were being garnished? Would I be able to assure her that these books had not been returned? How could I gain her confidence and cooperation to successfully resolve the problem?

I dialed the phone. After pleasantries were exchanged, she mentioned she was unaware of the notices because her mail was often stolen and her email messages were intercepted and deleted before she could read them. She was also sure that she had returned the books. Finally, she confirmed my suspicion when she mentioned the financial stress she was experiencing since her paycheck had been garnished.

I commiserated with her, noting that it must be frustrating to have mail intercepted, and I empathized that it must be very difficult to live with the uncertainty of not knowing when it happens. Next, I confirmed that I was sure the books had not been returned as I had gone into the stacks and checked myself. I mentioned that if she would like to stop by the library, I could personally hand her the list of missing titles to ensure she received them. I noted that once the books were returned, we would inform collections and her wages would no longer be garnished. She was grateful for the solution and agreed to stop by to pick up the list. Shortly after receiving the list, she found and returned all of the books. Her account was credited.

Mindfully viewing the situation from the patron's perspective allowed me to empathize with how her mental illness affected her interpersonal interactions and possibly contributed to her financial difficulties. By engaging with her rather than dismissing her as a "crazy person," I was able to gain her confidence. When I assured her I wanted to help, I gained her cooperation. Problem solved.

> **Author Bio**
> Carol has served as access services librarian and an associate professor at Winona State University since 2013. During her sabbatical she took on the role of manager of reference services at Qatar National Library. While at Qatar National Library, Carol had the opportunity to integrate mindfulness, emotional intelligence and critical reflection into her work with the reference librarians. Carol earned an MLIS degree from Dominican University, River Hills, Illinois, a BA degree in Mass Communication, Journalism from Winona State University.

Reassurance

To embody the ideal of Reassurance, we use matched informality levels, appropriate and timely humor, and positive reinforcement to bolster someone else's confidence. These actions can look different in leadership depending on your own personality and leadership style. At the administrative level, informality and humor are not quite the same as in the classroom or in a research consultation. Leaders can be formal, quiet, and serious or enthusiastic, bombastic, and hilarious, but all leaders carry with them an authenticity that reassures everyone in the organization that the person at the top is doing the best they can for the greater good of their library.

360 Leadership Practice

There are a few things you can personally do to begin changing the culture of a library. Instead of matched informality, leaders can simply talk to everyone at the organization. Remind yourself that you are not better than anyone because you are the boss, and good ideas come from all corners of the organization. Stopping to chat or check in with people at different levels in many departments opens channels of communication that sometimes appear to be closed in top-down organizations. This relationship-building will serve you well if, or when, your organization is faced with a crisis, but it is also a way find out about tiny changes you can make that will bring about large-scale satisfaction.

When you are speaking with others, don't take yourself too seriously. You may not be the type to crack jokes and that's fine. Use your mindfulness training, though, to put others at ease. Understand that, no matter what your intentions might be, students or staff may be intimidated by administrators in general because of previous experiences with those in power. Set others at ease by smiling and saying hello if nothing else.

As you influence your culture with interpersonal communication, you can cause the greatest positive shift in your organization by taking action at the highest level. It's simple: do what you said you would do—and more. For 360 Librarians in leadership roles, Reassurance can hold the weight of policy behind it. After you complete the SWOT analysis and bring your team of influencers together to create new policies, continue to implement ideas, enact policies, and give people throughout your organization the power and agency to make their own decisions, as promised. When they do this, give credit. Celebrate good work, and communicate creative ideas within your organization and to the wider community. Trust your people, and let *them* reassure *you* when they rise to the challenge of solving your stickiest situation together.

ENDNOTES

1. Stephen Brookfield, *Becoming a Critically Reflective Teacher*, 1st ed. (San Francisco: Jossey-Bass, 1995).
2. Daniel Goleman and Matthew Lippincott, "Without Emotional Intelligence, Mindfulness Doesn't Work," *Harvard Business Review*, September 8, 2017, https://hbr.org/2017/09/sgc-what-really-makes-mindfulness-work.
3. Brent A. Scott et al., "A Daily Investigation of the Role of Manager Empathy on Employee Well-Being," *Organizational Behavior and Human Decision Processes* 113, no. 2 (November 2010), https://doi.org/10.1016/j.obhdp.2010.08.001.

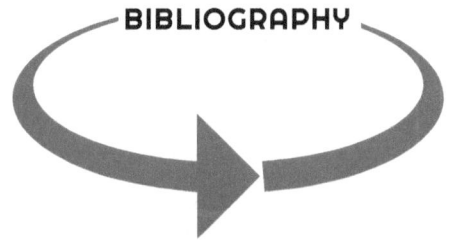

Bibliography

Accardi, Maria T., Emily Drabinski, and Alana Kumbier. *Critical Library Instruction: Theories and Methods*. Duluth: Library Juice Press, 2010.

Alkire, Sabina. "Subjective Quantitative Studies of Human Agency." *Social Indicators Research* 74, no. 1 (2005): 217–60.

Association of College and Research Libraries. *Framework for Information Literacy for Higher Education*. Association of College and Research Libraries. January 11, 2016. http://www.ala.org/acrl/standards/ilframework.

Baer, Andrea. "Critical Pedagogy, Critical Conversations: Expanding Dialogue About Critical Library Instruction Through the Lens of Composition and Rhetoric." *In the Library with the Lead Pipe*, December 7, 2016. Accessed September 1, 2017. http://www.inthelibrarywiththeleadpipe.org/2016/critical-conversations/.

Barbezat, Daniel, and Mirabai Bush. *Contemplative Practices in Higher Education: Powerful Methods to Transform Teaching and Learning*. San Francisco: Jossey-Bass, 2014.

Barrett, Lisa Feldman. *How Emotions are Made: The Secret Life of the Brain*. Boston: Houghton Mifflin Harcourt, 2017.

Batson, C. Daniel. "These Things Called Empathy: Eight Related but Distinct Phenomena." In *The Social Neuroscience of Empathy*, edited by Jean Decety and William Ickes, 3–15. Cambridge: MIT Press, 2009.

Boyatzis, Richard E., and Annie McKee. *Resonant Leadership: Renewing Yourself and Connecting with Others through Mindfulness, Hope, and Compassion*. Boston: Harvard Business School Press, 2005.

Bradberry, Travis, and Jean Greaves. *Emotional Intelligence 2.0: The World's Most Popular Emotional Intelligence Test*. San Diego: TalentSmart, 2009.

Brookfield, Stephen. *Becoming a Critically Reflective Teacher*. 1st ed. San Francisco: Jossey-Bass, 1995.

Bryson, Liz. "Humor Deficit: A Librarian's Guide to Being Funny and Competent." *Science & Technology Libraries* 28, no. 1–2 (August 2008): 87–99. https://doi.org/10.1080/01942620802096978.

Burgoon, Judee K., Laura K Guerrero, and Valerie Manusov. "Nonverbal Signals." In *The Sage Handbook of Interpersonal Communication*. 4th ed., edited by Mark L. Knapp and John A. Daly, 239–80. Thousand Oaks, CA: SAGE, 2011.

Burton, Neel. *Heaven and Hell: The Psychology of Emotions*. Oxford, England: Acheron Press, 2015.

Cabrera, Elizabeth F. "The Six Essentials of Workplace Positivity." *People & Strategy* 35, no. 1 (January 2012): 50–60.

Carter, Christina. "Save Your Marriage While Raising a Compassionate Child." *Greater Good*. Accessed May 21, 2017. https://greatergood.berkeley.edu/article/item/save_your_marriage_while_raising_a_compassionate_child.

Cooperrider, David L., and Diana Whitney. *Collaborating for Change: Appreciative Inquiry*. Williston, VT: Berrett-Koehler Publishers, 2000.

Daul-Elhindi, Carol A., and Tammi M. Owens. "Reference 360: A Holistic Approach to Reference Instruction." In *Teaching Reference Today: New Directions, Novel Approaches*, edited by Lisa A. Ellis, 98–117. Lanham, MD: Rowman & Littlefield, 2016.

David, Deborah Schoeberlein. *Mindful Teaching and Teaching Mindfulness: A Guide for Anyone Who Teaches Anything*. Somerville, MA: Wisdom Publications, 2009.

Davis, Dannielle Joy. "Mindfulness in Higher Education: Teaching, Learning, and Leadership." *International Journal of Religion & Spirituality in Society* 4, no. 3 (December 2014): 1–6.

Dewdney, Patricia, and Gillian Michell. "Oranges and Peaches: Understanding Communication Accidents in the Reference Interview." *RQ* 35, no. 4 (July 1996): 520–36.

Dewey, John. *How We Think: A Restatement of the Relation of Reflective Thinking to the Educative Process*. Boston: D. C. Heath and Company, 1933.

Diener, Ed, and Martin E. P. Seligman. "Very Happy People." *Psychological Science* 13, no. 1 (January 2002): 81–84.

Eggertson, Laura. "Lancet Retracts 12-Year-Old Article Linking Autism to MMR Vaccines." *CMAJ : Canadian Medical Association Journal* 182, no. 4 (March 9, 2010): E199–200. https://doi.org/10.1503/cmaj.109-3179.

Ekman, Paul. *Emotions Revealed: Recognizing Faces and Feelings to Improve Communication and Emotional Life*. New York: St. Martin's Griffin, 2003.

Esch, Tobias. "The Neurobiology of Meditation and Mindfulness." In *Meditation –Neuroscientific Approaches and Philosophical Implications, Studies in Neuroscience, Consciousness and Spirituality*, edited by Stefan Schmidt and Harald Walach, 153–74. Cham: Springer, 2014. https://doi.org/10.1007/978-3-319-01634-4_9, 158.

Foulk, Trevor, Andrew Woolum, and Amir Erez. "Catching Rudeness is Like Catching a Cold: The Contagion Effects of Low-Intensity Negative Behaviors." *Journal of Applied Psychology* 101, no. 1 (January 2016): 50–67.

Fujishin, Randy. *Creating Effective Groups: The Art of Small Group Communication*. 2nd ed. Lanham, MD: Rowman & Littlefield, 2007.

Furnham, Adrian, and Evgeniya Petrova. *Body Language in Business: Decoding the Signals*. Basingstoke, Hampshire, UK: Palgrave Macmillan, 2010.

George, Bill, Peter Sims, Andrew N. McLean, and Diana Mayer. "Discovering Your Authentic Leadership." *Harvard Business Review* 85, no. 2 (February 2007): 129–38.

Giesecke, Joan. "Emotional Intelligence." In *Academic Librarians as Emotionally Intelligent Leaders*, edited by Peter Hernon, Joan Giesecke, and Camila A. Alire, 1–10. Westport, CT: Libraries Unlimited, 2007.

Gilsa, Laura von, Dieter Zapf, Sandra Ohly, Kai Trumpold, and Sabine Machowski. "There is More Than Obeying Display Rules: Service Employees' Motives for Emotion Regulation in Customer Interactions." *European Journal of Work and Organizational Psychology 23, no. 6 (November 2014): 884–96. https://doi.org/10.1080/13 59432X.2013.839548.

Goffman, Erving. "On Face-Work: An Analysis of Ritual Elements in Social Interaction." *Psychiatry* 18, no. 3 (1955): 213–31.

Goleman, Daniel. *Emotional Intelligence: Why it Can Matter More than IQ*. New York: Bantam Books, 1997.

———. *Focus: The Hidden Driver of Excellence*. 1st ed. New York: Harper, 2013.

———. *Working with Emotional Intelligence*. New York: Bantam Books, 2000.

Goleman, Daniel, Richard Boyatzis, and Annie McKee. *Primal Leadership: Realizing the Power of Emotional Intelligence*. Boston: Harvard Business School Press, 2002.

———. "Primal Leadership: The Hidden Driver of Great Performance." *Harvard Business Review* 79, no. 11 (December 2001): 42–51.

———. *Primal Leadership: Unleashing the Power of Emotional Intelligence*. Boston: Harvard Business Review Press, 2013.

Goleman, Daniel, and Matthew Lippincott, "Without Emotional Intelligence, Mindfulness Doesn't Work." *Harvard Business Review*, September 8, 2017. https://hbr.org/2017/09/sgc-what-really-makes-mindfulness-work.

Gonzalez, Maria. *Mindful Leadership: The 9 Ways to Self-Awareness, Transforming Yourself and Inspiring Others*. Mississauga, Ontario: Jossey-Bass, 2012.

Hanh, Thich Nhat, and Katherine Weare. *Happy Teachers Change the World: A Guide for Cultivating Mindfulness in Education*. Berkeley, CA: Parallax Press, 2017.

Hanson, Rick. *Buddha's Brain: The Practical Neuroscience of Happiness, Love, and Wisdom*. Oakland, CA: New Harbinger Publications, 2009.

Hardenbrook, Joe. "Examining Library Spaces Through a Kindness Audit." *Mr. Library Dude* (blog). October 17, 2013. https://mrlibrarydude.wordpress.com/2013/10/17/examining-library-spaces-through-a-kindness-audit/.

Hardenbrook, Joe, and Jessica Olin. "Killing it With Kindness, Incorporating Sustainable Assessment Through Kindness Audits." (Presented at the Association of College and Research Libraries virtual conference, May 10, 2015).

Hatfield, Elaine, John T. Cacioppo, and Richard L. Rapson. *Emotional Contagion*. New York: Cambridge University Press, 1994.

Hume, David, David Fate Norton, and Mary J Norton. *A Treatise of Human Nature*. Oxford: Oxford University Press, 2000.

Jennings, Patricia A. *Mindfulness for Teachers: Simple Skills for Peace and Productivity in the Classroom*. New York: W. W. Norton & Company, 2015.

Kabat-Zinn, Jon. "The Attitude of Non-Judging." Mindfulness Training Online MBSR. Accessed August 20, 2017. https://www.youtube.com/watch?v=OwVkxcw1eZE.

———. *Full Catastrophe Living: Using the Wisdom of Your Body and Mind to Face Stress, Pain, and Illness*. New York: Bantam Books, 2013.

———. *Wherever You Go, There You Are: Mindfulness Meditation in Everyday Life*. New York: Hyperion, 1994.

Killingsworth, Matthew A., and Daniel T. Gilbert. "A Wandering Mind is an Unhappy Mind." *Science* 330, no. 6006 (2010): 932.

Langer, Ellen J. *Mindfulness*. Reading, MA: Addison-Wesley Pub. Co., 1989.

Larrivee, Barbara. *Authentic Classroom Management: Creating a Learning Community and Building Reflective Practice*. Upper Saddle River, NJ: Pearson, 2009.

Levy, David M. *Mindful Tech: How to Bring Balance to Our Digital Lives.* New Haven, CT: Yale University Press, 2016.

Maravelas, Anna. *How to Reduce Workplace Conflict and Stress: How Leaders and Their Employees Can Protect Their Sanity and Productivity from Tension and Turf Wars.* Franklin Lakes, NJ: Career Press, 2005.

Marturano, Janice. *Finding the Space to Lead: A Practical Guide to Mindful Leadership.* 1st ed. New York: Bloomsbury Press, 2014.

Matsumoto, David Ricky, Mark G. Frank, and Hyi Sung Hwang. "Reading People: Introduction to the World of Nonverbal Behavior." In *Nonverbal Communication: Science and Applications,* edited by David Ricky Matsumoto, Mark G. Frank, and Hyi Sung Hwang, 3–14. Los Angeles: SAGE, 2013.

Mellon, Constance A. "Attitudes: The Forgotten Dimension in Library Instruction." *Library Journal* 113, no. 14 (September 1, 1988): 137–39.

———. "Library Anxiety: A Grounded Theory and Its Development." *College & Research Libraries* 47, no. 2 (1986): 160–65. https://doi.org/10.5860/crl_47_02_160.

Mineo, Liz. "Good Genes are Nice, but Joy is Better." *Harvard Gazette.* April 11, 2017. http://news.harvard.edu/gazette/story/2017/04/over-nearly-80-years-harvard-study-has-been-showing-how-to-live-a-healthy-and-happy-life/.

Moniz, Richard, Joe Eshlemen, Jo Henry, Howard Slutzky, and Lisa Moniz. *The Mindful Librarian: Connecting the Practice of Mindfulness to Librarianship.* Waltham, MA: Chandos Publishing, 2016.

Neff, Kristin D. "Self-Compassion: An Alternative Conceptualization of a Healthy Attitude Toward Oneself." *Self and Identity* 2, no. 2 (2003): 85–101. https://doi.org/10.1080/15298860309032.

Owens, Tammi. "Communication, Face Saving, and Anxiety." *Internet References Services Quarterly* 18, no. 2 (September 2013): 139–68.

Padula, Alessandra. "Paralanguage." In *Encyclopedia of Communication Theory,* edited by Stephen W. Littlejohn and Karen A. Foss, 729–31. Los Angeles, CA: Sage, 2009.

Parkin, Steven S., Matthew S. Jarman, and Robin R. Vallacher. "On Being Mindful: What Do People Think They're Doing?" *Social and Personality Psychology Compass* 9, no. 1 (January 1, 2015): 31–44. https://doi.org/10.1111/spc3.12156.

Radford, Marie L. "Encountering Virtual Users: A Qualitative Investigation of Interpersonal Communication in Chat Reference." *Journal of the American Society for Information Science and Technology* 57, no. 8 (2006): 1046–59.

Radford, Marie L., Gary P. Radford, Lynn Silipigni Connaway, and Jocelyn A. DeAngelis. "On Virtual Face-Work: An Ethnography of Communication Approach to a Live Chat Reference Interaction." *The Library Quarterly* 81, no. 4 (October 2011): 431–53. https://doi.org/10.1086/661654.

Reale, Michelle. *Becoming a Reflective Librarian and Teacher: Strategies for Mindful Academic Practice.* Chicago: ALA Editions, 2017.

Romero, Eric J., and Kevin W. Cruthirds. "The Use of Humor in the Workplace." *Academy of Management Perspectives* 20, no. 2 (May 2006): 58–69.

Salovey, Peter, and John D. Mayer, "Emotional Intelligence." *Imagination, Cognition and Personality* 9, no. 3 (1990): 185–211.

Schön, Donald A. *The Reflective Practitioner: How Professionals Think in Action.* New York: Basic Books, 1983.

Scott, Brent A., Jason A. Colquitt, E. Layne Paddock, and Timothy A. Judge. "A Daily Investigation of the Role of Manager Empathy on Employee Well-Being." *Organizational Behavior and Human Decision Processes* 113, no. 2 (November 2010): 127–40. https://doi.org/10.1016/j.obhdp.2010.08.001.

Shapiro, Shauna, and Linda E. Carlson. *The Art and Science of Mindfulness: Integrating Mindfulness into Psychology and the Helping Professions.* Washington, DC: American Psychological Association, 2009.

Siegel, Daniel J. *The Mindful Brain: Reflection and Attunement in the Cultivation of Well-Being.* 1st ed. New York: W. W. Norton, 2007.

Smalley, Susan, and Diana Winston. "Is Mindfulness for You?" In *The Mindfulness Revolution: Leading Psychologists, Scientists, Artists, and Meditation Teachers on the Power of Mindfulness in Daily Life,* edited by Barry Boyce, 11–20. Boston: Shambhala, 2011.

Smith, Adam, and Knud Haakonssen. *The Theory of Moral Sentiments.* Cambridge, UK: Cambridge University Press, 2002.

Stearns, Peter N. "History of Emotions: Issues of Change and Impact." In *Handbook of Emotions,* 3rd ed., edited by Michael Lewis, Jeannette M. Haviland-Jones, and Lisa Feldman Barrett 17–31. New York: Guilford Press, 2008.

Stock, Matt. "The Three R's: Rapport, Relationship, and Reference." *The Reference Librarian* 51, no. 1 (2009): 45–52.

Tamir, Maya. "The Maturing Field of Emotion Regulation." *Emotion Review* 3, no. 1 (January 2011): 3–7. http://journals.sagepub.com/doi/abs/10.1177/1754073910388685?journalCode=.

Tolle, Eckhart. *A New Earth: Awakening to Your Life's Purpose.* New York: Plume, 2006.

Trager, George L. "Paralanguage: A First Approximation." *Studies in Linguistics* 13, no. 1-2 (1958): 1–12.

Vossler, Joshua J., and Scott Sheidlower. *Humor and Information Literacy: Practical Techniques for Library Instruction.* Santa Barbara, CA: Libraries Unlimited, 2011.

Waal, Frans B. M. de. "Putting the Altruism Back into Altruism: The Evolution of Empathy." *Annual Review of Psychology* 59, no. 1 (January 2008): 279–300. https://doi.org/10.1146/annurev.psych.59.103006.093625.

Walker, Billie E. "Using Humor in Library Instruction." *Reference Services Review* 34, no. 1 (2006): 117–28. https://doi.org/10.1108/00907320610648806.

Westbrook, Lynn. "Chat Reference Communication Patterns and Implications: Applying Politeness Theory." *Journal of Documentation* 63, no. 5 (2007): 638–58. https://doi.org/10.1108/00220410710827736.

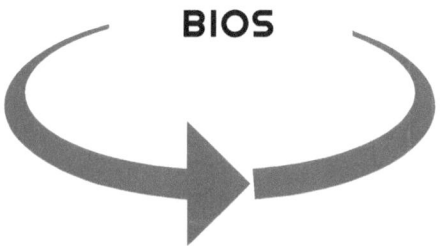

Author Biographies

Tammi M. Owens

Tammi is the outreach & instruction librarian and an associate professor at the University of Nebraska Omaha's Dr. C.C. and Mabel L. Criss Library. At Criss Library Tammi is responsible for coordinating, assessing, and continuously improving the first-year writing library information literacy program, leading partnerships with student learning communities, and hiring baby goats at least once a year (among other outreach events). She has written and presented at the regional and national level on such topics as library outreach and instruction, language use and user experience, gaming in libraries, and library tutorials. She holds BAs in Religious Studies and Art History from the University of Nebraska Omaha, an MA in Art History, and an MS in Library Science, both from the University of North Carolina-Chapel Hill. Tammi is a non-practicing Buddhist who re-establishes her yoga practice two or three times a year, and hopes her continual failures on these fronts gives others hope for themselves. Her meditative practice is in the fiber arts, as after eight years she has finally let her breath guide her as she spins yarn. She lives in a condo in Omaha with her husband, two cats, and four spinning wheels.

Carol A. Daul-Elhindi

Carol has served as a librarian and associate professor at Winona State University and as the manager of reference services at Qatar National Library. In her various professional roles, she has enjoyed the teaching and mentoring opportunities most. Her personal mindfulness meditation practice has allowed her to sort through her thoughts and feelings during some of the most difficult moments of her life. Her practice then seeped into her professional life serving as a way to handle stress, model authenticity, and improve relationships in the workplace. Carol earned an MLIS degree from Dominican University, River Hills, Illinois, a BA degree in Mass Communication, Journalism from Winona State University, and an AAS degree in Educational Interpreting for the Deaf from Northcentral Technical College, Wausau, WI. Carol and her husband split their time between their home in Winona and their villa in Doha.

Index

360 Framework, 3
    applying, 9–11
    in the classroom, 97–98
    ideals of, 4, 5, 85
    impact on workplace culture, 10
360 Journal exercises, 10, 18, 20, 31, 33, 50, 73, 77–79

A

ACRL (Association for College & Research Libraries) Information Literacy Immersion Programs, 3, 11n1
ACRL (Association for College & Research Libraries) *Framework for Information Literacy for Higher Education*, 85, 97
    Authority is Constructed and Contextual, 98, 107
    Information Creation as Process, 100
    Information Has Value, 107
    Research as Inquiry, 98, 103
    Scholarship as Conversation, 100, 103, 107
    Searching as Strategic Exploration, 110
action, 63–65
active listening, 48, 89. *See also* listening
agency
    human, 63–65
    of students, 93, 106–7, 109–10
assumptions
    affecting communication, 16
    automatic, 61
    awareness of, 19–21, 59, 104–5
    challenging 23, 102
    clarifying, 30, 34
    hegemonic, 9
    of organizational culture, 136
    questioning, 62, 120
    of students, 93, 102, 104–5
attention
    deliberate, 5
    divided, 13
    focused, 14, 15, 17, 18–19, 21, 22, 124
    mindful, 13
authenticity, 37, 41, 85, 92, 139
autobiographies, 9, 62, 67n11
avoidance behavior, 30
awareness
    conscious, 22
    focused, 15
    nonjudgmental, 16, 20–21
    open, 14
    self-, 8, 10, 30–32, 33
    See also Emotional Awareness

B

Barbezat, Daniel, 46
Barrett, Lisa Feldman, 33
Becoming a Critically Reflective Teacher (Brookfield), 9
bias, 101–2
blame, 30, 32, 46, 47
body language, 43–45, 134, 135
Boyatzis, Richard, 29, 70, 76
Bradberry, Travis, 30
brainstorming, 110–111
breathing
    breath counting, 16–17, 22
    breathing rate, 44
    focused, 16–17, 88–89
    and mindfulness, 15–16, 133
Brookfield, Stephen, 8–9, 60, 62, 131, 136
burnout, avoiding, 3, 86
Bush, Mirabai, 46

C

Cabrera, Elizabeth, 77
calming techniques, 17, 70, 89
Center for Mindfulness in Medicine, Healthcare, and Society, 6
centering devices, 17, 88
Chenevey, Liz, 88–90
clarity, 5, 6, 17, 21, 22, 23, 50
colleagues
    experiences of, 9, 67n11
    listening to, 134
communication
    authentic, 19–21, 48, 55
    back-channel, 44–45, 48
    deliberate two-way, 4, 41–42, 49–52, 91–92, 102, 134–35
    deliberately informal, 71–74
    face-to-face, 126
    improving, 27
    between librarians and students, 4
    during meetings, 46, 49, 51–52
    nonverbal, 41, 42–46, 47, 50, 91, 102, 126
    online, 126
    paralanguage, 47–48, 71–72
    verbal, 45, 47, 91
    See also Engaged Communication
compassion, 3, 14, 22, 23, 27, 34, 46, 70, 76, 78, 91, 98, 124, 131, 134
    self-, 20, 23, 56, 57, 70–71, 79
confirmation bias, 98, 101, 102
conscious living, 5. *See also* mindfulness
creativity, 23
critical feedback, 19–20
critical pedagogy, 64
critical reflection, 4, 8–9
    lenses for engagement, 9, 67n11
    cultural barriers to overcome, 131, 136
cultural barriers, 131, 136
curiosity, 20, 32, 47, 49, 58, 85, 88

D

Daul-Elhindi, Carol, 137–39
David, Deborah Schoeberlein, 6, 22
Davis, Dannielle Joy, 6–7
decentering, 64, 120
deep listening, 41, 42, 46–49, 50, 102, 104–5, 119, 135. *See also* listening
desk chair meditation, 20–21
De-Stress Fest, 122
Dewey, John, 8
Diener, Ed, 77
distractions, 13, 14, 22, 47, 50–51, 88
Doucette, Wendy, 129–30

E

eating, mindful, 18
ego-response, 64, 73
Ekman, Paul, 33, 44
Ellis, Lisa A., 4
email
    about hot issues, 126
    limiting engagement with, 125–26
Emotional Awareness, 4, 27–28, 56
    in information literacy classrooms, 100–102
    integrating, 37–38
    and leadership, 134
    in outreach and marketing, 116–18
    practicing, 29–36
    and student reference consultations, 90–91
    and technology, 125–26
    See also emotions
emotional intelligence, 3, 4, 7–10,

27–29, 35, 37, 69, 85, 98
and the ability to read people, 44
in the classroom, 100
five dimensions of, 8
in the workplace, 132
emotional labor, 30, 32
emotional language, 118
emotions
assessing, 32–34
and emotional state, 100–101
construction of, 33
neuroscience and competencies of, 69–71
noticing, 30–32
positive, 77
reacting to, 35–36, 134
regulation of, 29, 35–36
science and psychology of, 28–29
self-assessment of, 33
six basic, 33
See also emotional awareness; emotional intelligence; emotional language
Empathetic Reflection and Action, 4, 55–56
action, 63–65
and emotional awareness, 30
empathy, 56–59
in information literacy classrooms, 106–10
integrating, 65–66
and leadership, 135–39
in outreach and marketing, 120–21
reflection, 59–63
and student reference consultations, 92–93
and technology, 127
empathy, 8, 27, 34, 44, 55, 56–59
affective, 56, 66n2
cognitive, 56, 66n2
deep, 70
defined, 56
self-, 57
empathy reflex, 57–59
Engaged Communication, 4, 31, 41–42, 56
and emotional awareness, 30
in information literacy classrooms, 102–6
and leadership, 134–35
nonverbal, 42–46
in outreach and marketing, 119–20
and student reference consultations, 91–92
and technology, 126
engagement
authentic, 3
emotional, 125
empathetic, 60
focused, 50
interconnected, 42
mindful, 31, 44
purposeful, 4
structured, 103
with technology, 126
Esch, Tobias, 14
eye contact, 44, 45

F

facial expressions, 43–44
feedback, 10
candid, 33
critical, 19–20
expectation of, 69
positive, 79
filter bubbles, 102

G

gaze, 43

George, Bill, 37
gestures, 41, 43–44
Giesecke, Joan, 34
goals, 11
    communicative, 43
    inspirational, 79
    professional, 66
Goleman, Daniel, 7–8, 27, 28–29, 33, 35, 70
Gonzalez, Maria, 76

H

Hart, Molly, 117–18
Hatfield, Elaine, 56
Hermodson, Amy, 105–6
Human Library movement, 119–20
Hume, David, 56
humor, 74–75, 94

I

inclusiveness, 121
informality, 94, 139
    deliberate, 71–74, 94
    in emails and chats, 128
information literacy classroom, 97–98
    Emotional Awareness in, 100–102
    Empathetic Reflection and Action in, 106–10
    Engaged Communication in, 102–6
    Mindful Practice in, 98–99
    mindfulness in, 105–6
    Reassurance in, 110–12
    and technology, 105
information literacy skills, 91
intelligence
    practical, 8
    social, 7
    See also emotional intelligence
intelligence quotient (IQ), 8
intentions, 22, 62, 133
interpersonal limbic regulation, 70
introspection, single-pointed, 6
IQ (intelligence quotient), 8

J

journal exercises 10, 91, 125. *See also* 360 Journal exercises

K

Kabat-Zinn, Jon, 6, 15, 16, 20
kindness audit, 115–16

L

Langer, Ellen, 6
leadership
    360 Librarian techniques, 131–40
    authentic, 37, 71
    emotional, 29, 91
    Emotional Awareness in, 134
    Empathetic Reflection and Action in, 135–39
    Engaged Communication in, 134–35
    leading with the heart, 37
    mindful, 22–23
    Mindful Practice in, 132–33
    Reassurance in, 139–40
Levy, David M., 125
librarianship
    academic, 9–10
    critically reflective, 3
library anxiety, 77, 87, 100
listening
    active, 48, 89
    to colleagues, 134

concentrated, 31
deep, 41, 42, 46–49, 50, 102, 104–5, 119, 135
emotionally aware, 47
empathetic, 36, 57, 72
with focus, 92
to patrons, 73

M

Maravelas, Anna, 30, 34
marketing techniques, 85. *See also* outreach and marketing
Marturano, Janice R., 22–23
Mayer, John D., 7, 27, 28
MBSR (Mindfulness-Based Stress Reduction), 6, 20
McKee, Annie, 29, 70, 76
meditation, 14, 15, 17, 18, 20
mind mapping, 110–11
Mindful Practice, 4, 13–14, 56
    becoming an authentic communicator, 19–21
    and breathing, 15–17
    developing, 15–21
    and emotional awareness, 30
    in information literacy classrooms, 98–99
    integrating, 22–23
    and leadership, 132–33
    and letting go of the mind, 18–19
    in outreach and marketing, 115–16
    remaining in the moment, 16–19
    structures and relationships, 14–15
    and student reference consultations, 88–90
    and technology, 124
    See also Mindfulness
mindful service ethic, 89–90
Mindful Tech (Levy), 125
mindfulness, 3, 4, 5–7
    aspects of, 6
    defined, 5
    in higher education, 7
    in information literacy classrooms, 105–6
    misconceptions surrounding, 7
    and reassurance, 139
    See also Mindful Practice; writing, mindful
Mindfulness-Based Stress Reduction (MBSR), 6, 20

N

Neff, Kristin D., 57
negative self-talk, 23, 57, 76, 94
negativity, 57, 76, 134, 136
negativity bias, 76–77
neuroscience of emotion, 69–71

O

online communities, 126
outreach and marketing, 113–14
    Emotional Awareness in, 116–18
    Empathetic Reflection and Action in, 120–21
    Engaged Communication in, 119–20
    Mindful Practice in, 115–16
    planning, 114–15
    Reassurance in, 121–22

P

paralanguage, 47–48, 71–72
phones, disconnecting from, 124–26, 128
positive affirmations, 80

positive reinforcement, 76–80
posture, 43–44
practical intelligence, 8

R

Reale, Michelle, 60
Reassurance, 4, 69
    and deliberate informality, 71–74, 94
    and emotional awareness, 30
    and humor, 74–76, 94
    in information literacy classrooms, 110–12
    integrating, 80
    and leadership, 139–40
    and the neuroscience of emotion, 69–71
    in outreach and marketing, 121–22
    and positive reinforcement, 76–80, 94
    practice of, 71–80
    and student reference consultations, 93–95
    and technology, 128–30
reference desk, 4, 32, 34, 59, 75, 88, 94
reflection, 59–63, 64, 67n11
reflective thinking, 8. *See also* Critical Reflection
relationality, 15
relationships 23
    authentic, 69
    building, 76–77
    cultivating, 14–15
    dynamics in, 62
    meaningful, 37
    with online communities, 126
    strengthening, 27
    in the workplace, 66, 77–78
resilience, 85

S

Salovey, Peter, 7, 27, 28
self-awareness, 8, 10, 30–32, 33. *See also* awareness
self-compassion, 20, 23, 56, 57, 71, 79. *See also* compassion
self-confidence, 38, 41, 70–71
self-control, 28, 38
self-empathy, 57. *See also* empathy
self-regulation, 8
Seligman, Martin E. P., 77
Sheidlower, Scott, 74
Smalley, Susan L., 5
Smith, Adam, 56
social competence, 37, 57, 44, 70
social intelligence, 7
social skills, 8, 29
source material, 92, 93, 105–9, 111
student consultations, 87
    Emotional Awareness in, 90–91
    Empathetic Reflection and Action in, 92–93
    Engaged Communication in, 91–92
    Mindful Practice in, 88–90
    Reassurance in, 93–94
students
    anxious, 87, 100
    consulting with, 87–94
    eyes of, 9, 67n11
SWOT (Strengths, Weaknesses, Opportunities, Threats) analysis, 135, 137, 140

T

Tamir, Maya, 28
Teaching Reference Today (Ellis), 4
teamwork, 109–10
    in outreach and marketing, 114–15

technology
- and 360 Librarian practice, 123–24
- Emotional Awareness in, 125–26
- emotional connections to, 85–86
- Empathetic Reflection and Action in, 127
- Engaged Communication in, 126
- engaging and disengaging with, 85–86, 123–24
- and information literacy, 105, 123–24
- Mindful Practice in, 124
- reactions to, 127
- Reassurance in, 128–30

theoretical literature, 9, 67n11
therapy dogs, 122
Trager, George, 71–72
Turtle Island Student Organization, 117, 120

V

vocal qualifiers, 72
vocalizations, 71, 72
voice qualities, 72
voice set, 72
voices, 103–4
Vossler, Joshua J., 71–74

W

Wakefield, Andrew, 107
Westbrook, Lynn, 72
Wikipedia, 109–10
Winston, Diana, 5
workplace culture, 11, 22, 27, 41, 70
- changes to culture, 131–32, 133, 135, 136–37, 139–40
- culture of positivity, 77–78

workplace situations
- challenging, 131–32
- collaborative, 128, 139–40
- day-to-day, 11
- engaged, 41
- negative, 70–71, 80
- positive, 71
- relationships and, 11
- toxic, 32, 71

writing, mindful, 98–99

Z

zendoodles, 19
Zentangles, 19